CITIZEN
U.S.A

A 50 STATE ROAD T

CITIZEN U.S.A.

A 50 STATE ROAD TRIP

CITIZEN U.S.A.

A 50 STATE ROAD TRIP

Alexandra Pelosi

NEW AMERICAN LIBRARY

New American Library
Published by New American Library, a division of
Penguin Group (USA) Inc., 375 Hudson Street,
New York, New York 10014, USA
Penguin Group (Canada), 90 Eglinton Avenue East, Suite 700, Toronto,
Ontario M4P 2Y3, Canada (a division of Pearson Penguin Canada Inc.)
Penguin Books Ltd., 80 Strand, London WC2R 0RL, England
Penguin Ireland, 25 St. Stephen's Green, Dublin 2,
Ireland (a division of Penguin Books Ltd.)
Penguin Group (Australia), 250 Camberwell Road, Camberwell, Victoria 3124,
Australia (a division of Pearson Australia Group Pty. Ltd.)
Penguin Books India Pvt. Ltd., 11 Community Centre, Panchsheel Park,
New Delhi - 110 017, India
Penguin Group (NZ), 67 Apollo Drive, Rosedale, Auckland 0632,
New Zealand (a division of Pearson New Zealand Ltd.)
Penguin Books (South Africa) (Pty.) Ltd., 24 Sturdee Avenue,
Rosebank, Johannesburg 2196, South Africa

Penguin Books Ltd., Registered Offices:
80 Strand, London WC2R 0RL, England

First published by New American Library,
a division of Penguin Group (USA) Inc.

First Printing, June 2011
10 9 8 7 6 5 4 3 2 1

[NAL] REGISTERED TRADEMARK—MARCA REGISTRADA

LIBRARY OF CONGRESS CATALOGING-IN-PUBLICATION DATA:
Pelosi, Alexandra.
  Citizen USA/Alexandra Pelosi.
    p. cm.
  ISBN 978-0-451-23539-8
  1. Citizenship—United States. 2. Naturalization—United States. 3. United States—Social life and
customs. 4. American Dream. I. Title.
  JK1759.P375 2011
  323.60973—dc22   2011008811

Set in Minion
Designed by Pauline Neuwirth

Printed in the United States of America

contents

introduction

SEVEN YEARS AGO my husband, Michiel, was just one of the millions of immigrants who came to America legally. He was happy as a permanent resident alien, until the birth of our children. Then he realized he really wanted to belong to our country. So he started down the path to citizenship. On his journey to officially become an American citizen and to get to know his new country, we set out on a road trip across America to attend naturalization ceremonies in all fifty states to meet brand-new citizens to find out why they chose America.

We expected to see the cultural melting pot in the big cities, but we didn't expect to see it quite like we did in Tupelo, Mississippi, or Butte, Montana! In every state, we found a diverse collection of new Americans from over one hundred different countries. As we made our way from the Atlantic to the Pacific, we discovered that more and more immigrants are migrating to the suburbs. This confirms the 2010 U.S. Census Bureau data that shows immigrant populations rose more than 60 percent in areas of the country where they made up less than 5 percent of the population ten years ago.

America welcomes all types—Buddhist monks, homosexuals, scientists with PhDs, cancer patients, Obama haters, Obama lovers, Muslim imams, Christian missionaries, tech geniuses, movie directors, and a wrestler with his own action figure.

The one thing that new citizens seem to agree on is that those who were born in the U.S.A. don't realize how good we have it. Our new fellow countrymen appreciate the freedoms here considerably more than people who have been here for generations—and can help us see all that we take for granted: indoor plumbing, democracy, electricity, religious tolerance, free refills, uncensored Internet access, homeownership, funding for the arts, traffic laws, the option to go into debt, the freedom to have premarital sex, the right to bear arms, select your spouse, wear nail polish, read books, smoke, exercise as much as we like, and have as many children as we want. We can learn a lot from those who became American by choice.

Whether they came here via online dating, adoption, political asylum, student and work visas, or by swimming the Rio Grande (and overstaying long enough to be granted amnesty), they all came here to live an American dream. Although they have made themselves at home in their new country, our newest citizens still look at America with an outsider's perspective; they hold up a mirror to show us how we look as a nation.

At a time when it appears that this country is beset with problems—unemployment is at an all-time high, America's manufacturing base is eroding, the federal deficit is exploding, the poverty rate is at 17 percent, U.S. students' test scores rank below average in math and science literacy compared to other developed countries—immigrants from every other country on earth still flock here, because no matter how bad it gets here, it's still a heck of a lot better than most other places on earth.

In the seven films and two books I have made on the road across America, the one thing that I am still impressed by is how willing people are to welcome us into their homes and let us become a part of their lives. We are grateful to all the new Americans for sharing their stories, and for making this country a more interesting place to live! The best thing about this nation is that we welcome everyone. That diversity makes us great, and if we want to continue to be the greatest country on earth, we have to make sure the welcome mat continues to be out.

what are you bringing to this country?

I'm going to be the next Steve Jobs

PIMPREYA JUNE GEORGE
Born: Thailand
Home: Sioux Falls, South Dakota

WHEN I MOVED to Sioux Falls, South Dakota, I became somebody. I started a preschool called the Baan Dek Montessori. *Baan dek* means "children's house" in Thai, and it's the first and only accredited Montessori school in the state of South Dakota. I teach little kids everything about how to live together.

First I wanted to educate the community in Sioux Falls, South Dakota, and now I have an opportunity to educate the whole world. I created an app for the Apple Store and it's about Montessori material. My app is called Intro to Math, created by Montessorium. It teaches children about numbers and symbols and how to count and understand the symbol and the quantity. And my next app is called Intro to Letters. That one teaches kids about language and the sounds and the names of the letters.

I would love to be Steve Jobs. We recently got an e-mail from Steve Jobs at three o'clock in the morning. He e-mailed us about our apps and he encouraged us to keep dreaming, which is not dreaming anymore. It says, "I love what you are doing. Thank you. Let me know if we can help, Steve. Sent from my iPad."

When I grew up, I would never think that this is what I wanted to do. But in America, I saw the opportunity to become and live my dream. I have two dreams in my life. One is becoming a U.S. citizen and the second one is living an American dream. And I am actually [doing] both of them today.

I work on national security projects

MICHAEL FASSBENDER, PhD
Born: Germany
Home: Los Alamos, New Mexico

I'M A NUCLEAR chemist and I started working with Los Alamos National Laboratory ten years ago. This is a famous, premier nuclear weapons laboratory. It opens a lot of opportunities at Los Alamos if you continue to work as a United States citizen, because as a foreign national, you have limited access to certain information. And as a United States citizen, you have the opportunity to work on national security projects. In Germany I never had the opportunity to work on national security projects, because I don't think they are as elaborate and extensive as they are in the United States. If you come as a highly specialized, highly trained professional, you'll probably find an opportunity in the United States you wouldn't have in Europe.

In the times we live [in] today, it's very important to show a loyalty to a country, and the United States was the country that gave me the opportunity to develop my professional career. So I'm delighted to continue to work for the United States government. I think one has to make a decision of loyalty. And I made a decision of loyalty for the United States. Taking responsibility for your own existence is part of the naturalization. As we were going through the oath, you actually promise that you give up loyalties to your previous country. And that's what I did. So I am no longer a German citizen.

I'm going to be labeled "U.S. citizen" now, and no longer "working alien," which will even help me further doing important work for the nation. I'm going to be doing national security work for the United States. The U.S. needs people, not only me, but people like me. The strength of the United States is based on the skills and talents of people worldwide. And actually the National Laboratory is the world's greatest science protecting America. And I'm going to be part of it, and I am proud of it.

Jeanine, Michaela, Michael, and Kristin Fassbender—
Los Alamos, New Mexico.

I will find the cure for AIDS

DR. MOHAMAD F. JAMILUDDIN
Born: India
Home: Frederick, Maryland

I WANTED TO become an American so I can do the best research possible. Recently I got a patent in HIV research. I'm trying to develop a vaccine against HIV, and America does cutting-edge research. Particularly with the biotechnology research, America is number one. So I think I'll get the best opportunity to do research here, compared to my home country. Also I think America is in the best position to distribute the fruits of my research. My work got patented very fast, within two years. In India, I would not be able to have a patent at this age. In ten years I was able to have a patent and several publications, which wouldn't be possible in India. I did a postdoc at Cornell Medical College; it's one of the best in the world. And now whatever I learned I'm employing here. My company is developing a vaccine against TB, HIV, and malaria, and a number of other diseases. I'm particularly working on HIV/AIDS, and I think the technology and the other infrastructure available here make it possible to develop a vaccine against HIV. The citizenship and patent both happened at the same time.

It's recognition for our hard work, which we did here. We got citizenship based on our employment and our achievements. We work hard and our hard work has gotten recognition. It's kind of a reward for our hard work and whatever achievements we have made in our field. My wife and I both have PhDs. She was working on TB—host-pathogen relationships in tuberculosis. Since we are both in the same field, we both feel that this country is very good for us professionally. Here, you don't have to struggle for the essential items, like electricity and water—you have those things in abundance, so that gives me time to focus on my career and do something for society, for the world.

Dr. Mohamad F. Jamiluddin and Dr. Savita Prabhakar with their children.

I protect American soldiers

JEETESH KHEMANI
Born: India
Home: Bloomfield Hills, Michigan

I WORK FOR BAE Systems. They're a defense contractor. I build tanks and armored vehicles for the U.S. government. The soldiers are our customers, so we basically build things that would help our soldiers protect us. The U.S. is after terrorists or active terrorism. So that's our basic goal; our company's motto is, "We protect those who protect us." So we're protecting our American soldiers in the field. Our company is basically providing for the government, because they're trying to fight terrorism. So I'm proud of helping the American soldiers who are there protecting us.

I'm here to be a citizen, so this is my country now. And when I'm taking the oath, I'm not just taking an oath to get citizenship; I'm taking an oath and I'm going to abide by it, which means that I'm going to be protecting my country, which is going to be America. I will be helping America because this is my country. This is my soil now.

I really want to work for NASA, and for me to work for NASA, I have to be a citizen. It's just one of those "dorky" things to say: I want to be a rocket scientist. I want to build spaceships, and to go explore the deep unknown. I'd been hearing about NASA since I was a kid. I used to watch all these things on TV about space shuttles and about the technology that goes into it. I'm fascinated when I think about the speed of light. I want to be a part of R & D, research and development, and maybe design something . . . like one of those *Star Wars* movies, that you're standing there in a booth and "poof," the next second you're gone and you're ten thousand miles apart and you're there. It's really hard to imagine, but I'm sure Edison didn't know that there's something known as a "lightbulb," but he did it.

The fact that America was able to send someone to the moon, I think that is an amazing thing in itself that no one else has done other than America. My American dream would be to work hard and be a part of NASA and not just work there, but actually make a difference. Maybe change the way they work things. Maybe be a part of an amazing technology that's going to change the world, that's going to be part of history.

I keep the streets safe

HENRY BETHAM
Born: Samoa
Home: Ewa Beach, Hawaii

I AM A correctional officer at the Oahu Correctional Community Center. I uphold the law and keep the public safe. I am here to help my fellow man. I contribute to America by doing this job, keeping the streets safe, keeping the bad guys in. My job is to protect the public from people who are making bad choices with drugs and all that. I have been protecting the public for nineteen years. This kind of work, dealing with inmates, isn't cut out for everyone. I maintain security, monitor inmates; we have different programs for them—like rehabilitation. There is good in everyone; some people made the wrong choices and we are there to help them get back on a straight path, so to speak. I have to escort them to court, that type of stuff; it can get dangerous at times. I have felt threatened a lot. There are situations when you have to take inmates down if they are not obeying the laws of the facility. There are highs and lows; you just have to be prepared. We have training that keeps us ready for when the situation arises. My wife didn't want me to do this job. She was worried about my safety. But that's my job; I am committed to public safety. I am here to help everybody.

I saved America from Y2K

SANJEEV MALLICK
Born: India
Home: Salt Lake City, Utah

IMMIGRANTS HAVE A PR problem. Of course, the language is a problem. I can speak English very well because I learned it back in my country, but a lot of immigrants from other countries can't speak English very well, so they're always going to have a PR problem because they cannot really represent themselves.

The moment you hear the word "immigrant," there is a bad connotation to it. Let's admit it, right? I don't know how many people look at us walking down the street and think, "Oh, they're here legally." The word "immigrant" actually brings to people's mind somebody who is here illegally. As immigrants, we are lumped together. It's not fair for all of us who have gone through this huge process—it was expensive, it cost close to ten grand, and it took about twenty years. But we did it the right way. I think of this country as my country. I'm honored and proud to be a citizen of this country. But it is sad that we get lumped together with those who don't come here in a legal way.

Nobody likes the people who came here illegally; they broke the law, so the government keeps making more immigration laws, but they don't apply to the illegals, because they're breaking the law. All those laws actually apply to me, the legal citizen who follows the laws, so it makes it difficult for us, trying to follow all the rules.

America is letting me stay because I have the talent and the skill they need right now. America needs me. I'm contributing to America. I'm contributing my talent. I'm a skilled worker, and there are not enough people who can do the job I do. My wife and I were here during Y2K. We worked hours and hours trying to get the system ready. I know nothing happened, but that's because we worked so hard that nothing happened. And then we stayed here. In the technology world, there are not enough people to do the job. Nobody gives you a job for charity. The businesses don't run charities.

Sanjeev Mallick with his family.

WHAT ARE YOU BRINGING TO THIS COUNTRY?

I employ Americans!

AUSTIN NWOKO
Born: Nigeria
Home: Houston, Texas

ANYBODY WHO NEEDS some insurance, come to Austin Nwoko State Farm and we'll take care of you! I own my own State Farm insurance agency and I have five employees here.

This is the country that gave me the opportunity to own a business. I put the American flag on my truck because I wanted to show my patriotism to the United States, to show that I love my country and that I am what I am today because of the country that I'm in.

Everything I do has my photo on it. Before I opened up, I asked an older African-American agent and he said, "I didn't want people to know what I looked like." But things have really changed since then. I'm a real Texan. I feel so much at home here. My wife is a full-blown Texan. I make fun of her every now and then 'cause that accent comes out and she starts really talking "country." I met my wife at work at

Walmart; we had a Walmart baby; he loves the store too. I feel like the all-American dad. My great-great-great-great-grandfather had the pleasure of having twenty-five wives, but for me, one American wife is enough.

I never feel any racism in Texas. My father-in-law actually is a hard-core Republican. I'm a Democrat myself, so it makes for interesting conversations. My mother-in-law got me this beautiful poster of Obama. And it said something about leadership and she's like, "Put it in your office." I just don't want to piss certain people off. Republicans buy insurance too.

In the olden days, people would come to America and change their name so they could fit in. When I first got here, the cabdriver happened to be African and he said something that stuck with me; he was like, "Your last name will prevent you from being successful here." But you have football players and basketball players with these ridiculous names like Hakeem Olajuwon; you would think, "Why don't you change your name so we can pronounce it?" But in today's America, the bottom line is my picture and my name brings intrigue, 'cause customers always ask, "Nwoko, where are you from?"

I make Americans beautiful!

DR. ABDEL FUSTOK
Born: Syria
Home: Houston, Texas

I'M A PLASTIC and reconstructive surgeon. The history of this specialty is really related to the United States of America in a very major way because of the wars and the injuries that happened during the wars and the desire to make the injured look normal.

Plastic surgery used to be for the elite, for the wealthy and famous, and then there was an explosion of aesthetic and cosmetic surgery. Now the secretary can do it, anybody can do it. People can go and borrow money to do it. They can borrow money to go buy a new car, they can borrow money to have a new nose, they can borrow money to have new ears, they can borrow money to have a new face, or change their face completely. The fact that anybody could do it is a uniquely American thing. The uniqueness of this country is that it is available, it is possible, and it's accepted. Here, we accept that if you want to change yourself to look different, if you want to have a different nose or a different face, it's acceptable.

I came to America because every single new study that I was reading was in English and was from the United States of America. Every single new book, every single new discovery was from here. I wanted to go to the source.

Once I got into the system I was treated like anybody else. If I were in France you have an old system; in a hospital you have first chief, second chief, third chief, and you are the lowest person on the totem pole—it is by seniority. You die before you get to anything. I would never have been able in France to be ahead of anybody else if they were French and I was a foreigner. There is no way. Here, once I was in, I was like anybody else. Here only my expertise, my energy, my hard work matter, not whether my name is Abdel or Jack or John. Only your hard work, your knowledge, your expertise will get you ahead of anybody else, not where you came from, not what your name is.

That is uniquely American.

When I applied to a plastic surgeon position I thought: *Why would they take me, a foreigner with a heavy accent, ahead of all these good-looking guys and gals that were my colleagues?* And they were all turned down. What counts the most is your knowledge and your expertise—what you bring to the table. You will not find that anywhere else in the world. That I know for a fact.

I built L.A.

DEMETRIO GALLARDO
Born: Mexico
Home: Upland, California

I'M NINETY-TWO YEARS old. I worked in construction my whole life; I built some of the most important buildings in the United States and some special government buildings. I was working hard for all my life. I am retired but I spent twenty-two years building up Los Angeles. When I was building the Federal Building, I thought, *I want to be a citizen of the United States.* The most special building I built is this [Los Angeles] Convention Center, where I am becoming a citizen.

I brought air guitar to America

CEDRIC DEVITT
Born: Ireland
Home: New York City

COURTESY OF MIRIAM DOAN

I GREW UP in an idyllic middle-class community of Dublin. After graduating from college, and unable to find work as an historian, I left for the United States with a winning green card lottery ticket under my arm.

Back then, the Irish were still considered a trustworthy bunch, so I landed a job as a doorman in a fancy co-op building on the Upper East Side of Manhattan, where I read a lot and dispensed dry cleaning and packages. As much as I enjoyed that, there were dreams to be fulfilled, and I soon fell into an advertising career, where for the last ten years I've been shaping campaigns for all types of great American brands.

But my true gift to the American people was introducing them to their fourth-favorite pastime—air guitar.

A friend and I started the U.S. Air Guitar Championships and subsequently brought the world of competitive air guitar to America. As predicted, the U.S. took to air guitar with the same passion it takes to most competitive sports, and in the first two years we came home with two world titles, firmly putting America back on the rock-'n'-roll map. A few years later we went on to make *Air Guitar Nation*, an award-winning feature-length documentary about the U.S. Air Guitar Championships. That's right, folks, a documentary about air guitar. Only in America.

I'll represent the U.S.A.!

TAYA LEONOVA
Born: Ukraine
Home: Eagan, Minnesota

Taya and her mom, Natalya.

I WOULD LIKE to get into the Olympics and get a gold medal for the U.S.A. I work very hard on it almost every day at my practices. Another dream I've had deep inside, since I was young: I would like to be an actress or model. My life's dream is to get a scholarship and get a very good education and get into Harvard or Yale. I would like to be a marine biologist.

My mom found a friend on the Internet and they got married and we moved here. That's how I ended up in Minnesota. I came to America with my mother to have a better life. Since I'm here, I do rhythmic gymnastics. In the Ukraine, we didn't have a lot of money, and here we have a better life. At first, I didn't know English, but I learned it really fast. I didn't know what to do most of the time when I started school, but I get it now.

NATALYA, TAYA'S MOTHER:

One day, I decided that I really wanted to go to another country for a better life, a better future for my daughter. And I met a very good guy. He took us to the United States. I didn't speak English. We didn't know, but we really, really wanted to have a nice family and to stay here. Language is not a problem; people, they can talk without language at all. You know, they have to understand each other in the head.

We came to America when Taya was four years old, and she started to go for rhythmic gymnastics. For six years I used to drive her forty miles to the gym three or four times a week. In Minnesota in wintertime it is very hard to drive so far with all the snow, so we finally moved closer to her gym and now she practices eleven miles from our house. She has practice three hours a day, from five thirty p.m. till eight thirty p.m., three or four or five times per week. She is at the seventh level at IGM (International Gymnastics of Minnesota). The sister of the owner of this school, Nellie Kim, is a five-time Olympic gold medalist in artistic gymnastics. This is the best place for Taya to reach her dream of being in the Olympics.

I am going for the gold

DENNIS OGBE
Born: Nigeria
Home: Louisville, Kentucky

I'M A PARALYMPIAN. For the past eight years I've been holding the U.S. record in shot put and discus in the Paralympic Games. For the Paralympic Games in Beijing in 2000, I was ranked number one in shot put and discus, but I couldn't compete for America because I didn't have my citizenship. Even my home country wanted me to come and compete for them, but with the politics and the unsanitary conditions I could not go back. I knew that one day my American dream was going to come true and that one day I was going to wear the American colors in the Paralympics.

In Nigeria I had an accident when I was three years old. The nurse was not well trained and she injected me in the wrong place in my bone. The needle broke and I was in a coma for three days. Coming out of the hospital they transported me like a sick baby to a big hospital, and there I contracted polio due to the unsanitary conditions. I was in a wheelchair and both my legs were paralyzed from my early teens going forward. That would never happen here.

Americans sometimes take America for granted and don't appreciate what they have. Those Americans need to go out to be humbled and see what's happening in real life. When you don't know where your next square meal is coming from or when you see your neighbor starving or dying or when you couldn't afford a basic necessity like drinking water or clean air, you are going to appreciate what you have, like a roof over your head, AC during the summer and heat during the winter. Back home, if you have any of that it's a privilege. If this ceremony was in Nigeria, I don't think they would have the power supplies throughout the ceremony: the lights would have gone off. When you come from that kind of society and you come to America, you can see that you are blessed already.

In my home country, before I left, I got a first-class degree. But I stayed almost four years with no job. I had no prospects of a job because I didn't have anybody high up in the government that would aid me to get a job. People that got a third-class degree are getting jobs left, right, and center because they know somebody up there. That is corruption. They don't take you for what you are, but in America that doesn't happen. Most of the things you get are based on merit. They look at you, see

what you've done, and your work talks for you. It's based on what you are as a person and what you know in your brain, how smart you are. It is not based on who you are and how much money you have in your pocket. Like me, my dad worked all his life, but at the end he had nothing to show for it. He died without having a house in his name. I don't want to live that life. I want to come, work hard, and see the proceeds. In America there is privilege for everybody. If you work hard, you're going to see the proceeds.

what do americans take for granted?

CHAPTER TWO

Clean Air

The first thing when I came to the U.S., I was impressed by the gorgeous blue skies, because there was no pollution. We took pictures and sent them to my parents. In India, there is a lot of pollution and it seems to me they don't really care.

MANDIRA (FROM INDIA)—CHEYENNE, WYOMING

Electricity

We were lucky if we could have power for ten minutes a day. In Kenya, maybe 10 percent of the people have electricity and everybody else does not.

JAHZARA (FROM KENYA)—ST. CLOUD, MINNESOTA

Air-conditioning

The first time I walked past a store in the summertime, a huge gust of cold air came at me and I never felt anything like it. I thought I was having hot flashes. Then my sister-in-law explained that every store in America is kept at 72 degrees. Americans always need to control the temperature so that they are always comfortable.

NELLI (FROM MALAWI)—ROCKY HILL, CONNECTICUT

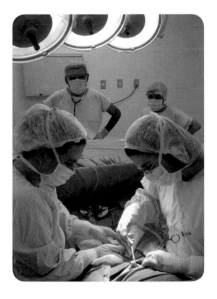

Health Care

We enjoy great benefits in terms of health benefits, medical, dental, as compared [to] the Philippines, [where] you have very limited coverage. Here, since I have a heart condition, I was diagnosed of having a rare congenital cardiac defect that requires me to have a pacemaker and an ICD. In the Philippines it's going to cost almost three million peso[s] and my insurance won't cover it. But here in the United States, as soon as I got the job, my insurance covered everything. I just need to pay a little bit co-pay. I really enjoy the benefits of my medical insurance.

**MEMETE (FROM THE PHILIPPINES)—
TRINITY, NORTH CAROLINA**

Internet

In my country they censor the Internet, so regular people don't have access to information. Here I enjoy the freedom of getting information. For example, when I called my mother to tell her that Liu Xiaobo was going to get the Nobel Peace Prize, she did not believe me. The Chinese government deleted all mentions of his name from all public domains, so when my mom went to Google it, all she got was error messages.

XIN (FROM CHINA)—SAN FRANCISCO, CALIFORNIA

Big Families

In China, they don't want you to have a lot of kids. They have the one-child policy so you can only have one child; if you have more kids, you get a huge ticket and you have to pay money. It's very expensive. If you don't pay, they deny citizenship.

DACI (FROM CHINA)—PHOENIX, ARIZONA

Free School

Everyone can go to school for free here. In my country, it costs money, and only the rich people can go to school; there is no such thing as public school.

SA'ALEH (FROM SOUTH AFRICA)—WOOSTER, OHIO

Free Speech

The fact that you can stand on the street corner with a poster of the president with a swastika on his forehead proves that this is a free country. Sure, it is in poor taste, but it's not against the law.

FATEHA (FROM SAUDI ARABIA)—EAU CLAIRE, WISCONSIN

No Torture

In Tibet, I was tortured. There are no basic human rights and no religious freedom there. After China's occupation, everything was destroyed and they brainwashed people so they could only study Chinese. They had a reeducation campaign. No freedom to preserve our own culture. I was a political activist and they put me in prison because I wanted Tibet to regain itself as an independent country. If you are a political activist against the Chinese occupation, you'll get tortured. Here they don't torture; they say you can't torture in America. So that's good.

TENZIN (FROM TIBET)—SAN FRANCISCO, CALIFORNIA

No Caste System

People who were born here don't realize that there are no social classes. In a lot of countries, if you're not born into a certain social class, it doesn't matter what you do; you're going to get held back. Here, it doesn't matter who you are, where you came from. If you work hard, you can really achieve anything that you want. This is the only country that would have ever allowed all of us to live our dreams, and to be whoever we wanted to be with no restrictions. This country says, "Of course you can do it!" As long as you put in the hard work, and you put your heart and soul in your dreams, then you can really make anything happen.

GLORIA ESTEFAN (FROM CUBA)—MIAMI, FLORIDA

Women Are People Too!

This country treats me like an equal. In Korea, women are always second; men always come first. When a boy is born, they have a celebration in the house, with a red paper lantern. Party if it's a boy! If it's a girl, nothing! You say nothing. As a woman you feel like a second-rate citizen, and here they treat me equal.

CHONG (FROM KOREA)—WILMINGTON, DELAWARE

Citizenship

I was born in Yemen but I am Jewish, so I was denied citizenship at birth. If you are anywhere in the Middle East and you are Jewish, they will not give you citizenship. America is the first country to grant me citizenship.

SAHAR (FROM YEMEN)—HOLLAND, MICHIGAN

Water

ROY CORREIA
Born: Portugal
Home: Bellingham, Massachusetts

I'M IN CHARGE of the water and sewer division of Ashland, Massachusetts. I make sure the water's clean, pure, and people can drink it. Water is a luxury; people don't realize it—they take it for granted. You turn on a faucet and the water's there. Nobody thinks anything of it.

The funny thing is, everyone complains about their water bill; people complain if the water pressure is low, and when the pipe breaks and we shut the water off in a neighborhood for, like, twenty minutes, I get about thirty phone calls demanding that the water be turned back on.

In a lot of foreign countries, people still go down to the rivers and get water. Where I'm from, water is hard to come by; you had to grab your jug and you walk a half a mile down to the river, and get it right out of the side of a mountain. And you had to go grab it every day, four or five times a day. It was not filtered; you took your chances with it. You could have sediment in it, sand, grit, little bits of pebble, algae, anything. And when that riverbed went dry, you had to hope it rained.

Here we treat it. We make sure you're getting the best possible water. And you need it! You've got to have water for cooking, cleaning, bathing, filling your pool, washing your car, and what if there is a fire? You can run out of electricity and light a candle or have a flashlight. You can run out of gas in your house and cook in a fireplace. But you run out of water, you can't cook, you can't stay sanitarily clean, you can't grow gardens, you can't grow trees without water, and that means no oxygen. Water is a gift. Water is life. We take water for granted, like anything else, until it's gone.

"Water is a luxury; people don't realize it— they take it for granted."

Land

MARIA THERESA DOWNS
Born: United Kingdom
Home: Great Falls, Montana

IN AMERICA, YOU have the right to purchase your own land. In Great Britain, you'll never own your own land. The queen owns the land. You might own the house that the land sits on, but the queen will always own the land; you have to just lease the land from the queen. She owns everything. She is the queen of the land. And you have to go with that.

Food (other than corn bread)

HILE CORRI
Born: Albania
Home: Jacksonville, Florida

IN MY COUNTRY I grew up like a slave. I worked my entire life for nothing. In communism, they give you bread. My entire life, we ate just corn bread. Nothing else. And that sounds ridiculous, but it's true. My entire life, I ate just corn bread; you cannot have another bread. It's like I don't believe for myself what kind of life I passed. My life was miserable. And I can tell all of American people they have to grow up and to say God bless America, because this country, it's unique in the earth for everything.

Here everything is like paradise. You can eat American food or Chinese food or Italian food. It's whatever you want, you can have. Because it's America. It's the best country in the earth. You want to eat pizza, you can eat pizza. You want pasta, you can have pasta. You want cake, you can find everything you want in this country. I prefer steak; it's my favorite. And Greek salad.

Free refills

MARTIN ASPIN
Born: United Kingdom
Home: Kennesaw, Georgia

BEING ABLE TO refill your soda is a dream for people all over the world. You can just buy a small cup and keep refilling it—and even share it! With the free refills, you don't have to keep paying for them, so you can actually spend more of your money on college. Back home, you have to pay for refills, and on top of that, they don't use ice. In England, all you get is one cube; they serve all the drinks at room temperature. Here you get like a whole glass full of ice.

WHAT DO AMERICANS TAKE FOR GRANTED?---

Debt

AEREE KIM
Born: Korea
Home: Metairie, Louisiana

THE BEST PART about this country is that it's given me an opportunity to go to school and to buy a house. In America, you can go to college even if you don't have the money; you can get student loans; you can go even if you can't afford it. There aren't things like that in Korea. In Korea, I could never go to college, because you have to pay up front. There are no student loans. If you don't have thirty thousand dollars to go to school, you couldn't ask the government, "Oh, can I take out a loan for thirty thousand dollars and pay it back once I'm done in four years?" I think that's one thing that people here take for granted.

Also, I was able to buy a house. I was fortunate to get my condo before the age of thirty because of the first-time home buyer program. You don't have that kind of opportunity in other countries. If I lived in Korea I wouldn't be able to afford a house unless I saved up for the past ten to twelve years of working.

Now I have student loans up to my eyeballs and I have a mortgage note, but at least I have something to show for that debt. Debt is probably the worst part of my life, because I have so much debt, but I have a house, I have a college degree, I have a job that I like that gives me a paycheck, because it's a blessing in disguise. Nobody wants to have debt, but that debt has given me stuff.

"In America, you can go to college even if you don't have the money. . . . In Korea, I could never go to college because you have to pay up front."

Free roaming

ABDUL AND ZAKI
Born: Jordan
Home: Arcadia, California

ABDUL:

Here you are treated as a complete human being. You can voice your opinion; you can even call the president and tell him, "You're a liar." In Jordan, you cannot even dream of thinking about such things. In Jordan, human beings are not treated as human beings. If you are dealing with any government authority over there they treat you like a dog; it's a subhuman treatment. You have to beg for mercy to get them to treat you well, because if you act like "This is my right," you're gone. You're going to be in a jail begging for mercy [for them] to let you go, until you say, "I'm sorry. I didn't mean it."

For seventy years I lived in Jordan. I was in the Jordanian military for over thirty-five years, and now I want to spend the rest of my life in America, because living here as a human being gives me so much power. You Americans don't see that. You don't feel it because you've been living here.

ZAKI:

In Jordan, you have a lot of checkpoints within the city. So wherever you go they stop you at night and say, "Give me your ID"; "Where are you going?"; "What are you doing here?" There's a lot of checks wherever you go. They tell you it's for the safety of the public, to prevent crime, but actually, it's to monitor people.

Think about it like this. At every major intersection in L.A. you have a police checkpoint where, at night, they can just stop people and question them about their whereabouts, where are they coming [from], where are they going, and what they're doing. They question you in a way that you would feel like you're a suspect.

Back in 2008, I visited my mom before she died, and I was stopped. I was going out at night with a couple of friends, about eleven o'clock, and they stopped us. There was a checkpoint and I gave them my California ID; I didn't have anything else. They checked the others and the officer was actually harassing one of the guys: "What are you doing here?"; "Where are you working?"; "What do you do?"; "Where do you live?" I thought it was absolutely ridiculous and I told the guys that and they said, "We are used to it."

You feel like you're in a dictatorship environment. You are watched and constantly harassed. So you are always in fear of being put in prison somewhere where your family doesn't know where you are. That's how they practice their dominance and control over the people, to make sure you understand that they are in control.

You feel vulnerable. I didn't know how much dictatorship we had over there. We knew it was an oppressive type of system. I didn't know how bad it was until I came over here and I made the comparison between the two and realized, "Wow, people over there really don't know what freedom is." They really don't understand. I really feel sorry for the people over there. There is no democracy. Zip. Zero. Zilch. The difference between Jordan and America is like comparing hell and heaven.

A lot of people may not tell you this stuff because they feel if they go back to visit, they'll get prosecuted. So you may not hear what I'm saying that often. If they see this on TV over there, they will say, "Okay, we need to get this guy." And they will try to come after me. So now that I talked to you, I can't go back.

Voluntary military service

SIVAN LAVY HOGAN
Born: Israel
Home: Tarzana, California

Sivan Lavy Hogan with her husband, Chris.

HERE, IF YOU'RE American, right after high school, you can do whatever you want. You can enjoy finishing high school and getting your bachelor's or travel the world, and I think it's really nice here that if you go to the army, it's voluntarily. In Israel, when you finish high school, they take you straight to the army and you have to go. It's mandatory; everyone has to serve their country. Girls included. You just graduated high school and you want to go and get your degree or travel the world, but they take the best years of your life, eighteen to twenty-one.

Israel is constantly in a war. It's not the most peaceful place to live. You can go on the bus and the next thing you know, the bus can get exploded by a terrorist and you never go home. My mom's best friend went to work and she got on a bus and there was a terrorist there and he bombed and killed everyone on the bus. You go to a school or the malls, or everywhere you go, they check your bags before they let you go in any public places, because they're afraid you might carry a bomb that will kill people.

Kissing in public

HELEN HENDERSON
Born: Malaysia
Home: Denville, New Jersey

THERE ARE A lot of restrictions where I come from. If you're a Muslim you can't hold hands or kiss someone in public, and you can't have premarital sex; that is wholly illegal, and if you get caught by the police, you will go to a courthouse and they will either fine you or put you in jail. Having sex prior to getting married is illegal. There was a famous singer back in Malaysia who got caught in a hotel with someone who was not his wife and he ended up going to jail.

What's great about this country is that I can hang out at a bar and drink till I fall down dead drunk and no one's going to care about what I do. It's mind your own business. You can kiss and hug someone next to you. It's a great feeling that I can hold someone's hand and kiss him in public, and most people do here. No one can stop you. You can be naked and just do whatever you want and I don't think anyone can stop you because we have the rights here. You can practice any kind of premarital sex, or even holding hands, kissing, with a member of the opposite sex in public. And that's just great. I like to go out to bars and take advantage of my freedom!

Gay rights

HOSSEIN
Born: Iran
Home: Hillsdale, New Jersey

I'M A GAY man. I cannot go back to Iran because of my sexual orientation. I had no choice. When I came here and I realized I'm gay, I had to seek asylum. The one main strategy for dictators like Ahmadinejad to make us invisible is by saying homosexuals don't exist. What he does, and many other countries also do, is they basically claim that we don't exist.

In Iran and also in a number of countries in the Middle East, sodomy is a crime punishable by death. So homosexuals are penalized. They are not allowed to have access to work. They are not allowed to attend universities. They are kicked out from their families. They are disowned by their own family. It's not only the law; it is the society and the culture that tries to ignore you and get rid of you as soon as they can because they think that you are a disgrace to the society.

And as long as you don't talk about it, you are an accomplice. When you start talking about your issues, then you have power over them. Then you can make people accountable. Then you can seek justice and demand your rights. This is something that I learned in this country. The LGBT movement in this country showed me that despite all of the problems, you have to stand up. And I think that's what I appreciate about the United States, the movement within the civil society and the encouragement by the civil society to stand up for your rights. What I appreciate most about this country, specifically for the gay and lesbian rights, is the fact that the gays and lesbians started to organize among themselves. And over the past thirty or forty years, they moved from this marginalized position to the mainstream human rights and civil rights movement. And now talking about LGBT rights is considered to be an acceptable topic. And I think that people in other countries have to also think about the ways that they can bring the issue of homophobia, of persecution of gay and lesbians to the mainstream and use this model in order to demand their rights and speak about their own pains.

I am married. We had our ceremony in New Jersey. My partner is an American. The U.S. government does not recognize us. The state of New Jersey does recognize us, but the federal government does not recognize us as partners and so we have no rights.

Love marriages

MEENAL PERIANNAN
Born: India
Home: Springboro, Ohio

BACK IN INDIA, my husband and I never met before our marriage. So we met, even though we are in the twentieth century, and all that; we married before we ever met each other. My parents met with his parents and his parents met with me and that's it, we got married.

When you sign up for arranged marriage it means that you accept the person, whom you don't even know, with full confidence because it's not the person that you're trusting; it's your parents that you're trusting that this guy is the right person for you. You first sign up and then you fall in love with the person. In America, you fall in love and then you get signed up and you get married.

In India, we always are bound to be with our parents until we are twenty-four or twenty-five years old. The parents will support us the whole time until we get married. When it comes to marriage, we say, "Okay, we're bound by you. Whatever you

Meenal with her husband, Palaniappan Chinnakaruppan, and their daughter, Remya Palani.

feel is right for us, you do it for us." So we just give our life to them because they give the life to us. And that's one of the reasons why we sign up for arranged marriages and we say, "Okay, my dad and my mom are going to choose the right person that suits me," because they know me from my birth till twenty-seven years, and they know who I am. So you accept the person as they are and then you start falling in love with that person.

Whereas, in America, it is the other way. You first make sure whether this person is going to be okay. Will this person be able to talk to me? Will this person take me out? Will he meet my requirements in the initial phase? And then you sign up: Okay, now I know this person is a suitable person for me and now I'm going to sign up for a marriage.

There are two ways. I know only one road; I don't know the other road. Now, if you know the other road, you will never know how my road is. So it is going to be a road not taken all the time for one person.

My daughter, she is five years old now, and twenty years down the road, it may not be the same culture and same thinking that parents would arrange for them. So it's going to be interesting to see how these kids are going to get married.

I'm open for a love marriage or arranged marriage. I believe that she could handle herself well and she's capable of doing things. She definitely will have the opportunity to say, "Okay, I like this guy and I like him because of such-and-such reason." America makes freethinkers.

Love American Style—
How did you meet your spouse?

1. He posted an ad on Craigslist that said, "I will marry you so you can become an American—I'm looking for a nice sweet Mexican girl who wants to become a legal citizen. Send me your photo." So I did.

    LOUISE (FROM MEXICO)—DALLAS, TEXAS

2. I met my wife at the Walmart. She was in the frozen-food aisle and I just walked right up to her and said, "Will you have lunch with me in the food court?"

    PHILIP (FROM SYRIA)—ARKADELPHIA, ARKANSAS

3. We met online through an agency in Miami. The meeting took place in Brazil. We visited because it was one of the precursors to what we had to do. He told me that he would be back for me but I didn't believe it. I didn't think he was going to come back. But he got a lawyer and started the process for the fiancé visa. I tried for my visa twice and I didn't have success, you know, because they are very, very selective. They said they didn't want people like me here. But they gave me a visa for three months and they said, "You need to marry in three months. If not, you need to go back to Brazil." So we went to the justice of the peace and we got married.

    SANDRA—ALBUQUERQUE, NEW MEXICO

4. We met at Trader Joe's. I went to Trader Joe's and I saw him and I thought he was the most handsome guy I've ever seen in my life. And I winked at him just to say, "Hey," you know, "you're such a good-looking guy," but I never thought I'd have a chance with him. I mean, look at him. And the next thing I know, he was standing, waiting for me, at the exit of Trader Joe's and he gave me his phone number and we've been together ever since. And now we rented an apartment right next to Trader Joe's and we live there.

    SIVAN (FROM ISRAEL)—CALIFORNIA

5. We met on Facebook. I had no idea I was going to have to go halfway around the world to pick her up.

ALEXA (FROM AFGHANISTAN)—ZEPHYRHILLS, FLORIDA

6. I met my husband at the bar. I walked in. He saw me. He grabbed my hand. He danced with me. And he said he's going to marry me. I didn't believe it and six months later, we got married. And now I'm becoming a citizen. That's my American fairy tale.

ZANETA (FROM SLOVAKIA)—WESTON, CONNECTICUT

7. I was on the Internet looking for an American husband. I knew that if I could meet a man on the Internet I could have a better life. I didn't really care what he looked like or anything like that; I just wanted to come to America.

ALEKSANDRA (FROM BELARUS)—HOLLAND, MICHIGAN

8. I was walking down the street in Acapulco and met this girl who was from Lincoln, Nebraska. We met, we spent about a day together, and she said, "I'm going to go back to Lincoln to get a law degree." And I said, "Well, I'll come visit," and I did. And I've been here seventeen years.

PETER (FROM BERMUDA)—LINCOLN, NEBRASKA

9. We met here at the Department of Homeland Security. I was in line waiting to fill out my paperwork and he was standing right behind me. I asked him for a pen and he asked for my number, and the rest is all documented in my USCIS profile.

LUKA (FROM UZBEKISTAN)—NEWARK, NEW JERSEY

10. I came to America to marry a very handsome and nice American man. I met my husband through a global Pinoy [Filipino] chat room. He had a "log in" name called "USAMAN," and I considered him as a God-sent gift to me, because I was asking God if He could just send me somebody that would love me for the rest of my life. Lots of my friends met their spouses through the Internet. It's really so amazing how the Internet is changing America.

ABIGAIL (FROM THE PHILIPPINES)—BRUCE, MISSISSIPPI

WHAT DO AMERICANS TAKE FOR GRANTED?

Family life

MIAO JIN SANDEL
Born: China
Home: Sacramento, California

IN CHINA, THEY have a one-child policy. After 1982, you only can have one child. I'm the first generation of the birth-control policy. When you're pregnant in China, you will have to go to the government to get a license to give birth. You have to have a license to give birth first, and then your child is born; then you have to give a birth license and a birth certificate to the government office to get a citizenship for the kids. That's how it works.

If you get pregnant again, the child that's born doesn't get Chinese citizenship. Your neighbors could turn you in. [Your child] can't really go to public school, and you'll have a hard time finding a job. If you have more than one kid and you have money, then you just pay money to buy the citizenship. They call it "punishment" money.

Miao Jin Sandel and her family.

Also the society is different. Like in China, all your friends go to work; everybody you socialize and get together with is from the work or working. I don't really know any moms' clubs or playgroups, like those kinds of things. In America, it's easier; we have our own playgroup and we have "moms' club" for us to go to hang out, to let the kids have friends. In China, most of the young ladies are working. And there is really no "stay-home" mom; probably only really rich people do that. So all the grandparents are taking care of the kids.

I'm a stay-home mom and I spend time with my kids, taking care of my kids. There's no such thing as a stay-home mother except for the really rich people. If I was in China right now, I would be working and my parents would be taking care of my kids. When a baby is born, after three months, I'll have to go back to work. And then the grandparents are taking care of the kids. That's what all the friends I grew up [with] in China are doing right now.

"In America, it's easier. . . . In China, there is really no 'stay-home' mom."

Child-abuse laws

SAJAN PRADHAN
Born: Nepal
Home: Woodbridge, Virginia

I LIKE IT here 'cause you don't see people getting killed. There's a lot of killings in Nepal. It's easy to get killed in Nepal. People just kill each other for no apparent reason. You see people getting killed all the time.

In school in Nepal, the teachers are allowed to hit the students. I remember getting beaten in school for no apparent reason. You get beaten just 'cause you didn't do your homework or something. Or just 'cause, like, you said a wrong answer; the teacher can just throw something at you. Or if you fall asleep in class, you know how they have the erasers? The chalkboard erasers, they were made out of wood, and the teacher would just throw it at you. I've seen my friends in Nepal get their heads split open by an eraser. So teachers are allowed to hit students whenever they want. Even the principal hits the students. Teachers could beat you when they felt like it. And you can't do anything about it 'cause they don't have a law that says you can't hit a kid in Nepal.

There's no such thing as child abuse in Nepal. Parents can beat their kids if they want. I feel safer here 'cause I don't get beaten by my teacher, and my parents can't hit me no more. It's a great thing. And I guess, like, the cops actually do their job, and they protect us from getting killed. And kids don't have guns. In Nepal, you just see kids running around with guns. It's just so easy to get ahold of a gun there. There's no such thing as "you have to have a license" there. Like, as a kid, I could just go and shoot somebody. It's that easy. In Nepal, you could bribe a cop easily.

Like, say, if you kill a person, you just give them, like, a thousand rupees in Nepal, and they'll just be like, "Okay, go ahead with your day," or whatever. The cops will just let it go. Like, they shouldn't even be allowed to be called cops.

Here I feel safe. America isn't as dangerous, because you have cops everywhere. Here, cops do their job. They're loyal to their country. I like America because I don't get beaten by my teachers and my parents can't hit me no more.

Protection

GISELLA STOCK
Born: Peru
Home: Smyrna, Delaware

EVERYONE [IN AMERICA] follows the law and respects the law. In Peru, people don't follow the laws, unfortunately. Sad to say that whoever has money is the one who rules. They don't respect traffic rules. As a consequence of that there are many accidents. If a [policeman] stops somebody on the street, bad drivers can give them money and then they let them go. So there's not a law that they follow, and that's why it's so important for me to respect the Delaware state police troopers. In Peru, the people who have money are the ones who make the rules. And I believe that's not fair, because people who don't have money cannot be heard.

The reason I decided to come here was because my mother abused me, physically and mentally. And this was the country that accepted me. I was looking for peace and love and tranquillity, and I didn't want to be hurt anymore. If I stayed in Peru, my mother would have continued abusing me. There was no government agency that would help. I went to the police to report that abuse, but it was just written on a piece of paper but they didn't care.

I came with two hundred dollars. I got my passport and I became an au pair. Here the system protects me. That's why I wear this flag pin. Now I am a totally different person. I am absolutely happy. I have my husband, my wonderful son; I am an accountant and I can't ask for anything else. I am living the American dream. To me, my dream is to be happy and find peace. Success is also good, but if you're not happy, with all the money you have it's not worth it.

Personal safety

LIDA WISNER
Born: South Africa
Home: Wichita, Kansas

THE FIRST TIME I came to America, I walked into my friend's living room and I looked outside the window and there were, like, no bars, no fences, no barbed wire to keep you in or people out. I could see out the window; it didn't feel like a mini jail! For me, freedom means I can take my family around the block for a walk in the stroller and I don't have to be worried about being hijacked or about them—or all of us—just being taken. It's nice to have the freedom to go around the block, walk to the store, leave the door open, and let the air come in.

In South Africa, you don't do that. You pretty much lock up. When I came here, I didn't have to lock my car; I didn't have to hold on to my purse like someone's going to take it. It's like a weight off your shoulders. The freedom of having just that little bit of relaxation, not having the fear of always worrying about what the next person around the block is going to do to me. People here experience the freedom of the basics, whereas in South Africa you don't really have that freedom of the basics.

Growing up, we went through drills about what we would do if somebody set the house on fire. You know, run to the bathtub, get in there. Here, you just don't think, "Oh, what am I going to do if somebody comes in my house or sets my house on fire or throws tear gas or just attacks the house?" It's not something you grow up with. We had escape routes. We had to have certain things that, something happens to this person in your family, what are you going to do, where are you going to go? It was different.

That is freedom, to have no fear that somebody will attack you at any time. For me, it's not an occasional terrorist attack. Because nine/eleven was bad. A lot of people died. But in South Africa, a lot of people die on a daily basis because of the attacks. Every day you wake up and you're like, "I have to protect this; I have to do this because somebody can attack me on the way to work, on the way back from work." There's even a rule: After ten o'clock at night at the traffic light, if there's no cars, you can go, because you can get hijacked. You don't stop at a red light at night.

Here, I get in the car in the winter and I let it run to get hot. In South Africa, if you would let it run, as soon as you're in your house, it's gone. You might not even make it to your house, maybe. It's really nice to have the freedom of just doing stuff and not having the fear of somebody taking away what you have all the time. Yes, you have bad neighborhoods and good neighborhoods. But in South Africa, even if you live in the best neighborhood, high-class, you still have the same fear.

WHAT DO AMERICANS TAKE FOR GRANTED?---

Less red tape

ROMAN
Born: Russia
Home: Charlotte, North Carolina

I LIKE AMERICA better than Russia because it's much easier to get your ideas accomplished here. For example, I'll be opening a business and all I need is two pieces of paper typed and signed. In Russia, you have to go through a lot of commissions; you have to get it approved by the government, and it's just more paperwork—it's harder to do any business there. And it's much easier here to get a driver's license than there, because there you have to pass a medical exam and you have to pay a lot of money to do so. And you have to take a lot of classes. But here you just come and take the driving test and you're done. The biggest difference in Russia is when you want something done here you just go ahead and do it. And it's very easy. There, you have a lot of obstacles. I think it's a lot easier to get anything accomplished here. And it's much, much faster. For example, getting a driver's license or registering a business or starting a business. I think you can become a very, very big person here just from nothing.

First come, first served

ORANART NAMSUPAK
Born: Thailand
Home: Charleston, West Virginia

IN AMERICA, IT'S first come, first served. You just go by line. If you come first, you get served first. In Thailand there's too much corruption. I went to the Thai embassy to renew my visa and I stood there in the morning and waited all day. And I was standing there since the morning and people skipped right ahead of me because they know someone in there. And they just went ahead of me and I just didn't like it. I didn't think it was fair. It just upset me. 'Cause I was there all day and people just skipped right in front of me. I thought I should speak up, but over there it's not like a free-speech country. I wanted to say, "Hey, I was waiting all day, and why did people skip in front of me?" Here, they treat everyone nice and everyone pretty much follows the rules. The law is good and fair.

Ornant with her daughter, Amy.

The rule of law

OJULU A. OBALLA
Born: Ethiopia
Home: Sioux Falls, South Dakota

THE UNITED STATES is very stable politically. The rule of law is stable here. I like the way they govern the people. In Ethiopia the dictators abuse the citizens. People who are in the government don't care about their own people. I never voted in Ethiopia because they just rig the vote. It doesn't matter who you vote for; everybody is a dictator who will not accept the rule of the law or accept the rule of the Constitution. So it's a fake; it's a fake voting there. That's why a lot of new immigrants here don't vote, because voting didn't matter in their country.

"The rule of law is stable here."

An honest government

HANNA SANKO
Born: Ukraine
Home: Fisher Springs, Indiana

I'M AN ACCOUNTANT. I know that the taxes are not exactly the most popular thing, but as an economist I always try to put an economist hat on when I look at fiscal policy. We in Fisher Springs live in a place with the most wonderful library that offers a great variety of books, video games, music CDs, DVDs, videos, and great schools and to enjoy all these amenities, you have to know where the money is coming from. Obviously as taxpayers, we perhaps sometimes are reluctant about giving up the money, but the most important thing is that we realize, you know, where the money is going.

We get a printout with an exact number for that much money: That much of your taxes is going to the library; that much of your taxes are going to school or improving the landscape, or what have you. So this is probably one of the most visible and great differences between the Ukraine and the United States.

I know that during my early years in the Ukraine, I was blessed with a great education, which, by the way, was free. And I was blessed to be exposed to a lot of knowledge, fine arts, theater, that was all subsidized and it was very available. Now, here, if you go to an opera, you probably won't see that many people that one would call "underprivileged." And guess what? It's because it is just not available to them. I think it is just very sad, as I believe that, you know, each person is valuable to God. And I wish that something could be done to reach out to each particular person. In the Ukraine, the taxpayers do not know where their money is going to. Whereas here it seems to be very clear, very transparent. The budgets are all available for people to observe and analyze and understand what is going to be financed at what cost.

As an accountant and as a taxpayer I think this system is very fair, and people feel confident in their government, and overall I think it really improves the overall quality of the country, and the people's trust in democracy. I think the ability to trust your government is a very important thing. Not all the people realize that not every country is blessed to be able to trust their government, at least with things like taxes. I don't know that every country in the world is as blessed to be able to see a whole lot of integrity amongst people with authority, a whole lot of transparency. And I believe as an individual, as a Christian, it is important to trust your government.

I did not trust my government in the Ukraine. I think a lot of people from my country would agree with me that there were times when everybody really had to question the government and the taxes; the fiscal policies, the social policies, the budget, the handling of budget, was never a transparent thing, and I'm not sure it is now.

I think a lot of people from Ukraine were really not sure whether they could trust the government handling people's money. Once you're not honest with one thing, chances are you might not be honest with other things. I trust the American government. I think if you compare the American government to many other governments around the world, for that matter, I think this is probably the most trustworthy institution of people that I can think of. The Christian values, the common human values such as integrity and trust, seem to be important to a lot of politicians. Overall I very much trust the American government, and I believe that they have people's best interests in mind.

Hanna Sanko with her family.

Fair taxes

LINDSTON LINDBERG
Born: Brazil
Home: Indianapolis, Indiana

WHAT I LIKE most about the United States is the government. I believe here people are more serious about tax money. So if you pay, you know you're going to see whatever you pay in—you can see good schools; you can see good roads; you can see everything's clean and you can see the government and business working. In Brazil, we pay a higher tax than you guys pay here but you don't see the return—you don't see good roads; you don't see good schools. You have a tax for everything and they are supposed to use the tax to improve our country, but we really don't see it. I believe here if you pay your tax you should be happy that you see the return on your tax—you should be glad paying your tax here.

I think if you realize how much you're paying and how much you're getting back, you have a really good, secure system in terms of the police, the firemen, so if anything happens in your place, in ten or fifteen minutes, you have a cop in your house or you have the fire truck at your house to see what's going on. If you need to go to a government building, you have a nice place to go. In Brazil, we have everything but it doesn't work well. So I think you guys should feel lucky. You don't realize that all you're paying is going back to all these great things you have here.

Here you pay mostly your income tax and some product tax. In Brazil, you have tax for every little thing. You pay tax on every little thing that you can imagine. We pay probably around forty-two percent of our income. Also, the number of people who do not pay tax in Brazil is higher than here. I think the government has a good system to collect your tax. And here, people really pay the tax. In Brazil, we try not to pay tax because we know that all the money we put in the government, we don't see coming back. Most of the Americans that I know, they pay tax knowing that they're going to get something back.

The school bus and the post office

RAWAN BARGHOUT
Born: Jordan
Home: Browns Summit, North Carolina

WHEN I CAME to America, the thing that shocked me was that the school bus stopped and every car behind and in front of the school bus stopped to let the kids go to their house safely. This is the most impressive thing I noticed. In my country, there were so many accidents. When I went to school, I saw accidents because they don't care about the kids when they go from the school.

America is a very organized country. You have a system to go through. In order to get what you want, there's a process and this is good. Like the post office. America has a great, great post office. In my country, the post office is not great; sometimes it takes a month to get the letter, even if it's in the post office itself. My sister had her application from the embassy in the post office for a month and nobody notified her that it was waiting for her there. Sure, in the post office here there's a line, but it's organized.

You don't have to pay to get an "A"

MARGARITA HILLARD
Born: Kazakhstan
Home: Westbrook, Maine

THIS IS A great country because it allows people to go to school, pursue their dreams without actually having to worry about paying extra to get an "A." In Kazakhstan, there are things that can be worked out under the table, so you can get an "A" if you know the professor. Actually some of my friends now are coming to America to get their degrees here because the American degree is very valued in Kazakhstan, because everybody knows that if you're getting a degree here, you're really getting it because you're smart and you worked for it, and not because you put extra money in your professor's pocket.

Meritocracy

GHINA AND HASSAN ABUL-KHOUDOUD
Born: Lebanon
Home: Cavalier, North Dakota

IN THE UNITED States, if you don't know anybody, it's your hard work that gets you somewhere. It doesn't matter who you are the son of or the daughter of; you are yourself here. That's what made us come here and that's why we're raising our kids here. Hard work pays off in the United States. When you work really hard, the chances are that you probably will get to where you want to be. In a lot of places you can die working hard and you never get anywhere. Here you work hard full-heartedly, feeling that it's going to pay off because you're going to get your dream.

In other places, you work hard out of necessity, so you're going to survive, but that doesn't mean that you'll get what you're wishing for. Here all you have to do is go through the steps, jump through the hoops, go to the university, get your degree, and then you start working.

What struck me when I came to the United States is, for example, when I started my residency program, I found people who had done so many things and stopped and then they started, and then stopped, and they restarted. And people who are two or three times older than me, and still they decided to stop and start something new. If they hadn't believed that there's an opportunity for them to do that, they wouldn't have done it. In Lebanon, it's extremely hard to do that. You cannot just be a carpenter one day and then stop and decide you want to be a lawyer, 'cause the system, the social framework, makes it really hard for that person to do that; it holds you back; it ties your hands.

In the United States, there's always an opportunity; there's always a way; there's always somebody there who will help you figure out a way to fulfill your dream or to restart again from scratch.

The Abdul-Koudoud family.

No Russian roulette

SOFIA DOZMOROVA
Born: Russia
Home: Oklahoma City, Oklahoma

IN THE UNITED States, if you work hard, if you study hard, you will get what you deserve. I believe this 100 percent. You will become what you want to be. In Russia, it's like "Russian roulette." You can work hard, you can study hard, but it's not 100 percent you will get what you want. It's like a 90 to 10 percent chance, or fifty and fifty chance, but it's not 100 percent you will get what you want, even if you

work hard. In America, it's more clear. You have more chance to succeed. And it all depends on you. I like to have my future in my hands. It depends on me and what I am going to be and what I can do for my life. I don't depend on a man. I can depend on myself.

I came to the United States to get all the opportunities I deserve. I was given the opportunity to build my life as I want and as I see it. I go to Oklahoma Community College right now and I have a job and I can support myself. I can work hard and if I want to have something more, I will just work harder. Or I can go to university and get a new job and new profession. In Russia, I finished university, but it didn't mean I would get a good job; there is a lot of things that don't let you get what you want.

In the United States, you can look around and see so many people from so many different parts of the world who came together and are working hard to make their dreams come true. For us, it's our dream come true.

"If you work hard, if you study hard, you will get what you deserve. I believe this 100 percent."

Free will

LASZLONE EDIT FAZEKAS
Born: Hungary
Home: Anchorage, Alaska

WE FLED THE communist country of Hungary. There you go to work. You do the daily chores and do everything [that] you have to do, but you are not picking the things that you like to do. You're not associating with things that you like to do or a group of people that you like. You just have to follow the big crowd. Whatever your parents and your relatives and neighbors taught you, you can't get rid of that. That's synced into your brain; that's what's pushing you to get to work, to pay up and pay your bills. Whatever the government tells you to do, that's what you do and you always feel that they push you down. They don't let you do whatever you want to do. That's exactly the freedom that was missing under the communist government.

It's not that it was very bad living under a communist government, but now that we know how different the other life on the other side is, it was very bad, and now we realize it. Back then we knew that something else existed that helps you blossom into life. Not just financially, but as a human being. Without that, if you don't have the chance to experience it, you don't know what else is out there.

We knew that America was a free country. We knew that you could go to school, that you could work. That you could buy a car and have a phone. We never had a telephone while we lived in Hungary. It was all these luxuries. When we came here we'd never seen paper plates or paper cups. We never knew how the heck you could drink out of those things.

The thought started in my husband's head that if we can just do the same thing in a free country, look at what you can do. Not just financially, but also with your head, with your brain, everything is just different. We thought: *If we just can get out of here we can do the same type of work anywhere else, where nobody is going to push you down, where nobody's going to hold you back. Look at what you can become. Just to live freely. On the weekends you go out to that lake with your children and everything.*

So I went to the tourist agency and we bought a ticket to New York City for one week. We paid everything in cash, for the airfare and everything else. And our bosses and everybody said that, "Hey, these guys have been to Germany and they came back, so they are good comrades, let them go." They gave us a visa.

So we packed up our belongings in one suitcase in May of 1986. We arrived at JFK and we never went back until we were legal here in the United States. This is our eleventh year in Alaska, the great land of Alaska. We love it here.

Free agency

DUSANKA PANCEC WELLS
Born: Slovenia
Home: Boise, Idaho

IT WAS MY dream from the time I was a little girl that one day I would be American. I love the free agency that comes with being in America. The free agency, to me, means that nobody tells me what to do and what I can be, and what I can become. I can be whatever I want to be. I can make my own choices. And I don't have anybody telling me, "You're not smart enough to do this." Or, "You're not good enough to do this." I can do it.

I grew up in communism. And then it converted into socialism. And it's different in the way that you're just told from the time you're very little what your limits are and what you can become. It kind of grows with you. Everybody has a place in that society. And they tell you what your place is. It's not your choice. I think just

Dusanka Wells and her family.

the whole society is that way. It starts with your parents, because they're conditioned that way. And then you get it from the teachers, who say, "Oh, you can't become this because you don't have good enough grades." Or, "Oh, you're not very musical, so you can't sing or you can't play piano." The whole society is that way. It's like, "Yeah, you should go do this." I was fifteen years old when I started working in a big factory, because I was told because I came from the poor family that I couldn't do much with my life. You know, that I should be a "blue-collar worker." You are just almost doomed.

I left when I was twenty-five. I had some friends over here. They helped me; they sponsored me. I went to college in the United States. I am living my dream. I feel extremely blessed. I accomplished everything that I wanted to and I still have a lot of goals. And I know I can accomplish them still, because here the government is not involved with your life as much as they were over there in Slovenia, where I grew up. I wish my parents would come over here but they don't want to. I feel it is unfortunate that my mom can't experience what I experience and I wish she could.

I guess what I'll never get used to is people complaining constantly about something. I know that things are a little harder right now, but people are constantly complaining about how bad it is. We have everything that we want. We have beautiful homes; we have cars; we can do whatever we want to do. People are very spoiled here. Just taking things for granted. And I'm worried for my kids. I guess it's okay if you're a little spoiled. But when you take things for granted, then you don't appreciate what you have. I tell my children that what they have here is . . . they have a beautiful soil where they can grow as much as they want, as big as they want. And sometimes you don't realize that you're on the beautiful soil and you can grow.

Self-determination

EKIN PELLEGRINI
Born: Turkey
Home: Chesterfield, Missouri

IN TURKEY, IT'S more like somebody else chooses what we are supposed to do. For example, here, you go to a university, and then after studying for two years, the basic courses, you choose what you want to study. In Turkey, the system places us into something. I was placed into sociology. My husband was placed into mechanical engineering. The education departments tell you what to study. Here they let you choose, or they open up all the possibilities and then they let your creativity work into that. So that you pick what you want to be.

Here they say no too, but you don't have to listen to anybody who says no. In Turkey, when people say no you have to listen [to] them, whether it's your dad, it's your teacher, it's your manager—if they say no, it's done. You have to respect and you have to take the decision and move on. Here, if people say no, you don't have to listen, even if you're a five-year-old kid. You know, our son keeps saying, "Oh, I can make my own decisions. I'm five." Like, "Really?" In Turkey, he would never be able to say that. We would make the decisions for him and he would have to respect us.

We're both very career oriented, and if I was in Turkey, I wouldn't be able to do what I'm doing now; I mean, I'm a professor here, and the research opportunities are endless. In Turkey, your socioeconomic status matters. If you have a higher social status, it doesn't matter what age or what gender you are: You're accepted as an authority figure. We've had female prime ministers; we've had female leaders; it's really not an issue. So I guess here it's a flatter society. You could be born into any kind of family and you could still go to Harvard and do whatever you want to do in life. So I think the American dream does exist.

We had better conditions in Turkey. We had our families, a better financial situation, but we are more comfortable in this culture. Turkey is a very collectivistic society; you live as a collective. Your identity is shaped by the group. Here, your individual accomplishments—you are more important. It's more achievement oriented, more individualistic. So it's a better fit for us here, because we're more individualistic. For example, here, when you introduce yourself, you'll say, "Hi, my name is so-and-so. This is what I do." In Turkey, you don't even talk about your job when you introduce yourself. You don't see your job as an identity. So here, your individual identity, achievement, success, your job, is very important. In Turkey, which group you belong to is very important.

No dictators

NILDA GUERRA
Born: Cuba
Home: Tupelo, Mississippi

PEOPLE BORN IN America take this country and all their rights for granted. If you're born in this great country you think, "Everybody's like this." You have the mentality that every place is like this. When I would say to my kids, "In Cuba, you can't go to the mall and buy a video game. You can't go to the mall and buy a pair of jeans," they were like, "How do you live?" Because it's inconceivable. They can't wrap their minds around it.

Fidel used to refer to everyone that was not a communist as "worms, the scum of the earth, dirt." So our parents taught my sisters and I that we should be proud because we were "worms" and that was okay to be a worm. "But don't tell anybody that. That's our little secret inside our home." So my dad would say, "What are you girls?" And we'd wiggle our finger because that meant we were little worms. And we were very proud to be worms.

I think it's instilled in you. I remember being in school—we had our little red bandanna symbolizing communism. We had to say the Cuban anthem before school every morning, and it talks about being a communist. And it talks about giving your life up for communism and that would be a worthy cause. And we

would just say it. You had to say it. If you came out and spoke up against the government, you could get thrown in jail; they'll make your life a living hell.

Castro used to try to separate the families. To make himself look good, he would say, "Okay, you have to apply to leave," so it was like applying for a job; you couldn't just say, "Give me a ticket; we're leaving." The government had to grant you permission to leave. So when my parents got their letter saying my dad and my sister could go first and then my mother and my sister and I could go in a few months, they knew already. And they said, "No, thank you. Either we go together or we stay together." So they had to wait a whole year not knowing which way it was going to go. And then they got the magic letter saying all of you can leave together. So that's how we got out of Cuba.

There's not enough to go around, so we all had to get very little rations of everything. A family would get, like, a pound of meat for the week. When kids turn seven years old, the milk was taken away because the government decided kids were old enough and didn't need milk. It used to be where each family would get, like, a little booklet. Once a week you'd go into this place, I guess it was like a giant supermarket, but you don't go in to grab the things; you go in and give your little booklet to whoever is working. And they would open it up and say, "Okay, you're . . . you're due your ration of bread today, milk, meat. Here's your bread. Here's your milk. Here's your meat. Next." And that was the extent of your shopping experience in Cuba.

People did all kinds of stuff to survive. My aunt told me stories of people raising pigs in their apartments to fatten them up so they could eat them, and cut their vocal cords so they can't make noise and squeal, and just fattening them up so they could eat them. She also told me that one day, off of the freeway, somebody just set up a burger stand and she said the lines of cars were just a mile long, 'cause everybody wanted to get a burger. 'Cause that's unheard-of; you don't have burger places in Cuba. So somebody must have turned them in; everyone snitches on everyone. So the government showed up at the burger stand to investigate about the burgers and they found out the burgers were made of worms. So they were selling worm burgers.

And when Hurricane Katrina hit, I heard the people were getting drinking water from, like, puddles in the street, because it's survival of the fittest. Every day people make makeshift rafts to get out of there, 'cause they're at a point where they're like, "Well, we'll die trying or we'll make it to the United States." And 50 percent of them die in the ocean. Fifty percent make it; 50 percent die. Every day they're dying because it's freedom or death. And they choose to dive into shark-infested waters in the hope that the tide will float them this way.

When I was seven, my godmother was able to get out of Cuba and she would write my parents a letter. And she would get the real thin onionskin paper to write on, 'cause if the letter is even remotely thick, the government will just throw it away. They'll open it, read it, and throw it away. Your life is their life, not your life. And she would take the Wrigley's flat spearmint gums and she would tape three pieces, three sticks of gum on the paper, on the letter to my mom and dad. So when that letter came, we knew that there was a stick of gum in there for each one of us. And it was like Christmas. So we each got our stick of gum and we chewed it from morning till night. And when nighttime came, of course, it didn't taste like anything by then. But we were not going to throw that piece of gum out, 'cause that's all we had. So we'd take it and do like you're going to blow a bubble, and we'd take it out and fill it up with sugar, make a little sugar ball, and close it, and stick it in the freezer. And the next day we'd pop that right back in our mouths and we had gum until it literally disintegrated in our mouths and we swallowed it all.

So my life now is a dream. And kids don't realize that, especially. My kids are American citizens, so they've grown up not needing anything. And I tell them, like my son, one time his Game Boy was lost and I said, "Well, you need to look for it." And he was like, "It's okay, 'cause I can get another one when I really want one." And I chewed him out. I said, "Let me tell you something." I said, "That's not the way it works; you take care of what you have and appreciate it. And if that's your attitude, then you don't need to have another Game Boy."

Nilda with her father and sisters.

No government censorship

RUBY AND ROBIN YANG
Born: China
Home: Rapid City, South Dakota

IN CHINA, THEY don't let you go on Facebook or Google or YouTube. If you search up stuff, you get in trouble, 'cause they don't want you to, like, know about America. I think they just don't want any, like, bashings of the Chinese government. I'm, like, a Facebook addict. I go on it twenty-four/seven. If I had to go back to China, I'd probably just, like, crash. I don't know what I would do. They have their own Facebook for Chinese people, but I heard that it's really lame.

The government is everywhere. The government is controlling. It's, like, all-powerful. They don't want Chinese people to get too smart, I guess, and overthrow the government. I guess they want to hide Chinese secrets, make sure Americans don't get their hands on Chinese food, you know, like learn how to make their special fried rice.

In China, there is no teenage life. There is no social life. If we grew up in China, we'd probably be smarter, but we'd have a lot more stress, bags under the eyes every day. The school is so hard, too much pressure, too much competition. It's like college in, like, elementary school. School is easier here. We came here and everyone was still counting on their fingers, counting their toes, like, "I don't know how to multiply." When I first came here I felt like, "Wow." I didn't want to say it, but, like, everyone was a lot dumber than I thought. Like they were still not intellectually developed. But now, like, as we get older and stuff, people are starting to catch up. I feel really smart here because my mom said, like, "If you go back to China, you'll probably fail in school there. But you get to be top students here."

Also, in China, the teachers can spank you. Like, they can spank you for discipline. And you have school, like, six days a week, 'cause everyone wants their kids to be smart so they take them to weekend school on Saturday. It's mostly studying every day, studying, taking a bathroom break and an eating break and then studying, and sleeping for two hours. Here they let you learn other languages, like Spanish. And that's pretty cool. The focus is not just on education; it's pretty much making you a well-rounded person, 'cause they have clubs and sports and stuff, and they don't have that in China. We're going to college this fall, USD and the University of Vermont in Burlington. Whoo! Go, Catamarans!

We're Americanizing our parents; we force them to eat American food like meat loaf and pizza, 'cause I want to make them white. We help them assimilate to the culture by making them watch TV with us. We watch a lot of family TV together, like *The Office*, *Family Guy*, *Gilmore Girls*. The *Gilmore Girls* is about a girl who rebels against her family morals, and, like, she wants to go her own way, and my mom thinks that, since we're kind of rebelling against the Chinese tradition, we're kind of more Americanized, she thinks that show helps her to get more accustomed to what a parent should think and how they should respond to the kids not going on the way of the parents. My mom just loves it. She just, like, stays up nights and watches it. She's a TV addict.

What the Yang Twins Discovered in America

1. Fat people

The first thing my grandpa did when he came here was take a picture of someone's fat bottom and sent it back to China. They don't have fat "buttocks" in China. America has fat people. Like really fat people. Obese people. That's so mean. But it's true.

2. Fast food

Chinese food is, like, too healthy. I like going out for the occasional Taco John's. The fresh taste of West Mex, makes you say *olé*.

3. Squirrels and wildlife

They don't have squirrels or wildlife 'cause they eat everything in China, dogs included.

4. Hot guys

Oh, there's, like, no hot guys in China. That's bad. I'm into white guys. Just saying.

5. Tan people

Chinese people do not like to tan. That's why you see Asian people with umbrellas, 'cause they don't want to get tan. It's more youthful to be white.

6. White people

I went to Borders and there was a book called *Stuff White People Like*. At the end of it, you take a test and my white friend got 1 percent less than me; I thought that was kind of ironic.

7. Recycling

I learned to recycle here, to be eco-friendly and green. At college they have, like, four different trash cans; like, recycle plastics, trash, and then compost, so we're learning to give back to the community by recycling and making the earth more green. In China, they don't do that.

8. Summer vacation

Here they have long summer breaks. They don't have that in China; they have year-round school. So we're pretty lucky to be here. Hey, girls just want to have fun.

9. Cute clothes

In China, I wouldn't have all these cute clothes. Sorry, I had to add that. We're kind of, like, shopaholics. So we're pretty spoiled. Last weekend, my dad drove us all the way to the Mall of America. He spoiled us by taking us shopping, but he didn't complain at all.

MR. YANG: There's nothing to complain about as long as my daughters are happy.

what did you discover when you came to america?

CHAPTER THREE

Medicine

This country is so advanced medically. It's helped my family on certain occasions when they had medical issues; probably some of my family members wouldn't be here today if there wasn't a twenty-four-hour pharmacy around the corner from my house. The fact that drugs are so available, you can find any medicine in the grocery store for whatever ails you, makes this country unique.

RAMON (FROM SIERRA LEONE)—SAGINAW, MICHIGAN

Refrigerators

When we got to my sister's house the first thing she did was take us into the kitchen and she opened the fridge and I had never seen anything like it. I loved seeing all the food. Double doors with a built-in ice maker on the outside? I never dreamed of such a thing.

Now I have that fridge, and an extra fridge in the garage!

AUGUSTINE (FROM HAITI)—BUCKEYE, ARIZONA

Dishwashers

I'd never seen a dishwasher before I came to America, because under a communist government that was unknown.

TATIANA (FROM INDONESIA)—KOKOMO, INDIANA

Automatic doors

For the first time in my life I discovered a door that opened by itself. I never saw that before. I was petrified. I thought to myself, *Automatic doors? This is something out of science fiction.* This country is so advanced.

NAJIA (FROM TANZANIA)—MOODY POINT, MAINE

Staplers

The first day, when I got in the office to work, I actually didn't know how to use a stapler. When my boss said, "Okay, go staple this document," I could not do it. I didn't know what to do, so she had to show me from the beginning. I have a college education, but the struggle as an immigrant in the new society is with the very small things we have to learn.

BINH (FROM VIETNAM)—SAN FRANCISCO, CALIFORNIA

Doorbells

The first day I came to work, I didn't know how to ring the doorbell. I have a master's degree, I'm a geologist, but I did not know that you have to push the bell and it makes a sound. I didn't know that. So I just kept standing there.

LUONG (FROM VIETNAM)—SAN FRANCISCO, CALIFORNIA

Pizza delivery

The fact that I can pick up the phone and ask someone to bring a pizza and deliver it to my front door, still hot out of the oven, is the most remarkable thing I ever experienced. Sure, I have done it a thousand times, but I still can't believe it is possible. Did you know that this is the birthplace of Pizza Hut?

TIMUR (FROM MALI)—TALENT, OREGON

Cup holders and televisions built into the car

In my country cars are for transportation. Here, they are a destination in themselves. My minivan is more comfortable and well stocked than my house was in Guatemala. When I need to run some errands, I just throw my kids in the car and let them watch their favorite *Bob the Builder* DVD on TV. And when they get thirsty, they just reach for the juice in their cup holders.

**OLIVIA (FROM GUATEMALA)—
AMERICAN FALLS, IDAHO**

Cheap gas and liquor

When I first came down here, the one thing that I just couldn't get over is that you could fill your truck up for twenty dollars. In Canada that would run me a hundred dollars. The taxation on gas is just gigantic. And I could go buy a bottle of Crown Royal for about half of what a bottle of Crown Royal is in Canada, and it's made in Canada.

TOMMY (FROM CANADA)—SUGAR LAND, TEXAS

Drive-through everything

You can drive through the bank to get some cash and then go pick up any kind of fast food, coffee, or liquor and you never have to get out of your car!

WALTER (FROM OMAN)—BOW, NEW HAMPSHIRE

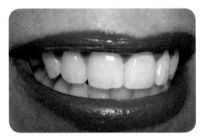

White teeth

In America, you see all these good teeth. In Europe, I never saw teeth like that. American smiles are superwhite, even whiter than white, and perfectly straight. Americans are obsessed with having perfect teeth. In the U.S. kids go to the orthodontist and get braces. In Italy no one goes to the dentist; I never went to the orthodontist.

LUCA (FROM ITALY)—NEW YORK, NEW YORK

The sale

I saw this ad for Best Buy that said, "Happy Hanukkah, Merry Christmas, *Feliz Navidad*, Happy Kwanzaa, *Feliz Día de Reyes*, Happy Eid al-Adha." They will say anything to get you into that store to buy a TV. What does the Muslim feast of sacrifice have to do with selling flat-screens?

AMIR (SAUDI ARABIA)—DETROIT, MICHIGAN

Toilet paper

I never heard of Kleenex and blowing your nose in paper and throwing it away. I literally had never heard of toilet paper. We used to wipe and blow our nose into rags and you washed them.

GENE SIMMONS (FROM ISRAEL)—BEVERLY HILLS, CALIFORNIA

The pursuit of happiness

ZEENATH JAHAN LARSEN
Born: Pakistan
Home: Brohard, West Virginia

IS THERE ANY country in the world that has it enshrined in the Constitution that you have the right to be happy? Any country? Once Pakistani boys had to go to Afghanistan to play football. And the Taliban were there at that time. The boys came out on the field in shorts and they were beaten up, because they were wearing shorts; they were not supposed to wear shorts. And the Pakistani government was silent. You expect your government to stand up for you, to protect you, but if they don't stand up for you, they don't protect you, what's the point of it all, then? If you hurt one hair on an American's head, the whole government of America, the whole State Department, they're at you. They're on you. So, you can't; nobody dares.

It's still very difficult for me to understand the real concept, the connotations of the word "freedom." My granddaughter, for the first time, she came to America. We took her to Virginia Beach. And she wouldn't take off her jeans. I said, "You've been to Thailand, so how did you swim in the sea there?" She said, "In my jeans." I said, "Well, you're not going to go in your jeans." I said, "I got a swimsuit," so I made her wear that, and she loved it. She was thrilled to bits about it, but the first day she wore that she was sort of feeling uncomfortable. She felt she was naked. She grew to like it, and then we took them to the Busch Gardens and the water gardens, and she and I are walking around in our swimsuits. And I said, "Padma, can you imagine? We are from Peshawar! Look at us here! People are on the beach; they could do what they please."

You can say, "I love my country," when your country and you share values. And the Pakistan of today is not the Pakistan I was born in or brought up in. The bottom line is that your country and you have to be on the same page where values are concerned, where principles are concerned. And if that is not the case, then you can be maybe born somewhere and brought up somewhere but you don't feel that same type of loyalty. Because loyalty comes to ideas, not to the earth, not to modern trees and hills.

The shopping experience

ANN SIMERA
Born: France
Home: Redmond, Washington

MOST THINGS ARE bigger in America than elsewhere. Everything is bigger here. Not just the fridges and the cars, portions at the restaurant, distances, houses, but everyday things. The first store we went to when we arrived here was Costco. I couldn't believe the size of the cart. My son was able to lie down completely in it to take his nap. After that, I always used to carry a pillow with me so he could nap while I did the shopping.

I was amazed at the size of the packaging. In Europe, the common size for milk and soda packages is one liter; here it's usually half a gallon, which is approximately twice as big. I was so impressed with the size of things that I began to measure everything to compare it to the size of French artifacts. I was amazed by the size of the toothpaste tube, bottle of wine, and tea package. The winner was the tube of paper towels. We really knew that something had changed for us when we were buying that, and now it would be hard to go back. This habit of measuring everything stayed with me for years; even after three years here, I was still comparing my newborn daughter to the size of things.

The feeling of being a VIP while shopping has never gone away, even after ten years, while the cashier is packing my stuff for me. I will always remember the first time with nostalgia. The cashier had just packed some coffee and a loaf of bread and then asked me if I needed help outside. What? I was almost offended by the question. Why was he thinking that I couldn't carry a small-weight grocery bag to my car? The first time I went back grocery shopping in France after two years in the U.S., my first reaction was to wait, arms crossed, in front of a puzzled cashier while the amount of stuff was piling on the counter. I got an angry look from everybody waiting in the line (the lines are always longer in France), and a rude comment woke me up, and I finally began to pack with frenzy.

It took me a while to get the paper-or-plastic question, and I have never used the help to go to my car, but one day I will, when I have completely gotten over the packing experience, just to keep the romance alive. Also, I have come to realize that when a cashier is giving you a compliment, for, let's say, your necklace, he really means that your necklace is pretty and he is not trying to flirt with you.

The return of goods is also a beauty in America. My American friend told me that you could return expensive cream, even if it's half-empty, because you have come to realize, after six months, that you don't like the scent. Or an open bottle of wine, worn shoes, stuff like that. The last time I had to return something in France, it was a schoolbook for my kids, with mixed-up pages; the pages were put in wrongly. I had to demonstrate to the sale lady that it was even not possible that I did it on purpose and that the errors were most likely coming from the print shop. I didn't get my money back, but I was able to do an exchange.

America is all about abundance! Like the oversize portions in restaurants. And the napkins! You can get as many as you want at the restaurant! It's there, in front of you, for free. You just don't get one on your tray; you are let alone with the entire box, and your kids can play a game of removing all of them to count how many there are, and nobody will say anything to you. Amazing.

The right to bear arms

TOMMY PILGRIM
Born: Canada
Home: Sugar Land, Texas

I'M AN AVID hunter. I'm an avid shooter. I enjoy shooting clay, skeet, target shooting, bow hunting. The ease of purchase of firearms in the U.S. compared to Canada was a real appeal to me. One of the very first things I did when I legally could was buy a target rifle that I wanted all my life and could never get. It's too big of a problem to get in Canada. And since then I've added to my collection and I really enjoy shooting sports. It's my hobby; it's what I love to do.

My daddy took me hunting from the time I was four. Since I was old enough to walk, I was out hunting with him. And to be able to share that with my own son now is pretty important to me, 'cause I lost my dad about six years ago and it's important to me to pass that on to my son, no matter what country I'm in.

Here in America it's just so much easier to enjoy those freedoms. Here there's different hunting. There's easier access to certain types of land, easier access to certain types of weapons, firearms, bow hunting, reloading, things I didn't even know I could do before. You could go and buy a firearm and go out and shoot it affordably. You could afford to buy a firearm. You could afford to buy ammunition to shoot your firearm because it didn't cost you a fortune to go do it. So you could enjoy those sports.

It's a lot easier to do those things here in America than it is to do [them] in Canada. You can have guns in Canada but you have to register them so that the government knows exactly what guns you have. Now, any American that owns guns would cringe at that statement, and I understand fully, because if they would decide one day, "Okay, you guys aren't going to have any more guns," then that's it. They can come take them all, 'cause they know what you have. Anybody who owns a firearm is going to fight any sort of registration. The Second Amendment gives them that right to have arms. And they shouldn't have to register them if they don't want to.

And I enjoy those liberties, and I have enjoyed them ever since I've been here. Here there are less restrictions. It's easier to buy sporting arms, easier to have sporting arms in your house. Canada restricts who can have them, who can buy them, when you can buy them, what kinds you can buy. We don't have that same oppression here as they have in Canada. I have four pistols and I probably have twelve or fifteen long guns if I sit down and count 'em. It's going to be hard to take my guns away.

If you take guns away or make it difficult for the American people to have guns you're only going to take guns away from legal citizens. Criminals are still going to have guns. As long as they make 'em, criminals are going to have 'em. So people should be able to defend themselves.

Entrepreneurship

HARINDERJIT S. AHLUWALIA
Born: India
Home: Fairfield, California

WHEN I CAME in this country, I started working in a 7-Eleven, a graveyard shift, twelve hours. I worked very hard. Then I opened one store and then I opened another store because it was successful. Only in America, I can do this kind of business. I could not open a cigarette store in my country. I am an Indian Sikh, and in our religion, we are totally tobacco prohibited. In our religion: no tobacco. In India, my community would not allow me and my conscience doesn't allow this kind of business. There is a restriction in my religion to smoking. I'm fifty-four, I never smoke, and I never drink. I never touched a pack of cigarettes in my life when I was in my country, but I have to do business; I can sell tobacco. I am a businessman.

My kids will not do this business; they are very sharp minded. My son, he just graduated premedical from the University of San Diego and next year he will go to medical school. My daughter, she just graduated from San Francisco State with a degree in criminal justice—she will work for an attorney. I give them a good education. They will choose their own careers.

A good place to start a business

TOMMY VOETEN
Born: The Netherlands
Home: New York, New York

IN AMERICA YOU can set up and incorporate your business within days and that is in big contrast with doing business in the Netherlands. Here, to start a corporation all you need is a lawyer—that's it. The incorporation of my business took one phone call from my lawyer's office to the IRS to retain a federal tax number, and my business was born that day, for under one thousand dollars. In the Netherlands, to incorporate would take at least three months and thirty thousand dollars. It would also involve hiring a lawyer, a notary, and an accountant; therefore it's a lot more complicated.

The U.S. makes it as easy as can be to start a business. Here it's simple and affordable, plus you don't start with a roadblock. In the Netherlands the incorporation of a business is similar to navigating an obstacle course: From day one you, the business owner, become a target for all sorts of taxes and fees from government agencies, from the beginning of your endeavor as an entrepreneur.

In the Netherlands, clients would have a hard time finding my company. However, in New York City, there you are, in the center of it all. The accessibility is priceless. There's also a noticeable difference in the drive and ambition here in the U.S. People get back to you in a timely manner and are eager to do business. The nine-to-five mentality, especially in my industry, does not exist here.

I design custom and innovative LED (sustainable) lighting products, specializing in the architectural and entertainment markets. For example, I was able to work on the U2 360° Tour: I designed a key lighting fixture called the U2BE. Perhaps the most exciting element of working on that tour was coming up with a custom solution for the circular LED-lit microphone, called the U2MIC, just for Bono. It's the only microphone of its kind. It hangs from a steel cable and allows for Bono's face to be illuminated while he swings from it around the stage. The microphone has been referred to as the crown jewel of the tour! I can say that the speed in which business is done in the U.S. has allowed me to grow my own business exponentially faster than I ever could in the Netherlands.

"The U.S. makes it as easy as can be to start a business."

You can do wine as you please

AGUSTIN HUNEEUS
Born: Chile
Home: Rutherford, California

JUST TO SPEAK of my area of expertise and where I've developed my life in this country, winemaking. Winemaking in America is free. We can plant vineyards wherever we want; we can plant whatever varieties we want. We can do wine as we please. There are no rules except, of course, fraud, which we wouldn't do in anyplace. But in Europe, most areas are constrained to certain regulations, certain plantings, certain varieties. Here, we can experiment with anything we want.

And it's beautiful because in America we respect tradition. But we review it. We look at it and if it has sense, if it makes some difference, if it somehow or other adds value, we keep it. But, if not, we change it. We are not tradition restrained, as in most other winegrowing areas in the world. And this has given American wines a tremendous advantage over Europe. The rest of the New World has learned from America that free enterprise is the way to develop wineries and wines.

In Europe, we would have been restrained as to what we can do. What varieties we could plant; what clones we could use; what distance; what management practices; those are all imposed by history, or whatever, but regulated. And, here, we had everything to choose from. We wanted to plant certain varieties in a certain row direction and make a certain style of wine. That is not open like that [in] Europe. And that's the beauty of the New World wines, led by the United States right now.

I think that the wine business in America would not exist if it were not for immigrants, because they are the ones who work the land and they like it, and know it, and I would say that a hundred percent of our vineyards around here are operated by Mexican immigrants. The permanent work in the vineyards requires technical expertise and hardy, consistent physical work that not everybody is willing to do. The proof is that right now, for example, our labor force here is a hundred percent foreign, immigrants, all legal, by the way.

We had to leave our country of origin for political reasons when we were still young. It never occurred to us to go to any other place but America. America was the place that would absorb people from all over the world and let them be whatever they could be. There was no other country in the world, and still is not, probably, any country that shares that mentality, that possibility.

The American dream is often spoken of as an economic sort of thing, but for us, the American dream was something quite different. The American dream was total freedom to become whatever you are; whatever you are intimately, released from

the typical bounds of societies in other countries that restrict you to a certain path related to your past history or to your family, or to your social position, or to your locality, even.

America doesn't limit you in that. You are free to be what you can be. And even though the economic dream today might be in jeopardy because of the economic situation, I think that that other part of the dream, the freedom to be whatever you can, is still there. We go back to Chile very often, and we go to other places and love it also. But that sense of total independence, total freedom, I think you will get that only in this society.

The most important difference between America and Chile is that the kids in Chile are being brought up to follow their predetermined path. Their education and their teaching, everything is dedicated to that very limited scenario that they're supposed to live within in Chile. My kids here are intercultural; they meet all walks of life and they study everything. It's a much broader bringing up than they would have in Chile; you are free to be what you can be. My grandchildren are being brought up with a much wider scope of life in terms of understanding the whole world, understanding multiracial integration that we have here, which is unique in the world. I think that's very rich.

I have three daughters and they don't care at all about the wine business. It's a difficult and very demanding business. I hoped to have given some of them the vocation, as I did my son Agustin, the vocation to keep doing this work. You know, this is not a one-generational thing, to take a piece of property, or multiple pieces of property, and develop wines that are the ultimate creation and the most beautiful that particular terrain can produce. That's a multigenerational thing.

Geodesic domes

PATRIZIA HERMINJARD-SMITH
Born: Switzerland
Home: Colorado Springs, Colorado

MY HOUSE IS an Arts and Crafts bungalow. It was built in 1908. This summer my husband built this geodesic dome that is our greenhouse. And it's got strawberries, squash, melons, our dinner salad, and pumpkins. It's an experiment. Our neighbors love it. They have a chicken coop, so we're going to trade some vegetables for some eggs.

We got a neighborhood beautification award. This isn't the richest area of town, and so they encourage people who try to do something to sort of beautify it. This neighborhood is wild. It really suits me, because all the homes are so individual and they say so much about each person that lives in them. It's something that's very foreign to me as a Swiss-born person. Switzerland's very quaint, very close together and particular about its rules. You wouldn't have the space to have your own little dome greenhouse.

One of the things that I really appreciate about America is its architecture and the space around its buildings and the largeness of the United States. We came to this country because there was space. There's just so much land and so much room to express yourself and build. It sounds a little trite, but you need space to live. You can buy a lot of land here. You can't buy land in Switzerland unless you're incredibly wealthy. I'm thirty-five and I own my own home and I live on a double lot, and that's just not possible in Switzerland for the average person. It's a very good life. I think a lot of people would envy us.

My mom gives me grief about not flying an American flag. I think she was concerned about the neighbors. Most people mistake the Swiss flag for the Red Cross. I think I would fly a Swiss flag in America because that's the other half of me that isn't here. And in Switzerland, I would probably fly an American flag because that's the part that is missing over there.

Here in Colorado Springs, things are less neat and less organized, and more based on individualism. In Switzerland you have very strict building codes. You have a desire to protect what they've had untouched by war for six hundred years. So they don't want their buildings to change. And I think that's what I love about America. I love the change, the potential for change, the desire for change, and I'm someone who thrives on the knowledge that I can change.

"We came to this country because there was space."

Honky-tonks

GÉZA KESZEI
Born: Hungary
Home: Lynn, Massachusetts

THE ONE THING they have in America that you won't find any other place is the honky-tonk, where you can go and dance to country music. I used to hang out in the honky-tonk, having a good time looking for girls. A honky-tonk doesn't look much different from a bar; it's noisier and livelier. People sing and drink and dance. Now that I'm American, I'll really fit in a honky-tonk.

America has the best country music in the world. When I came to this country, it was the "big band" era—Benny Goodman, Glenn Miller, Jimmy Dorsey, Eddie James; they were the best. But as time has gone by, I started listening to country music. I really like Patsy Cline. I like those sad songs.

I became American because my social life isn't too good. I hardly have any friends because everyone knew I wasn't an American citizen. I have been in United States since 1957 but I always was a second- or a third-class American. Nobody liked me because they knew that I wasn't American. I have trouble associating with people. I am becoming American because I would like to improve my social life. Before, when I was a so-called alien, they weren't really associating with me. They just think I'm strange to them, you know? I'm not one of them. Now I can say I'm one of the gang.

I need friends to socialize with, now that I'm getting older. I'm lonely now; since my wife died I'm all by myself. I was taking care of my wife for the last eight years 'cause I was her caregiver, and she passed away in July. Now I'm retired. I hardly see anybody. And I get lonely. I haven't been in a honky-tonk in I don't know how long, but maybe I'll drop in one of these days.

Disney World

TATIANA KORDIC
Born: U.S.S.R.
Home: St. Augustine, Florida

WHEN I WAS a young girl, all I really wanted was to visit Disney World. It was my dream, since I was in the U.S.S.R., the former U.S.S.R. I'd seen pictures from a girl that I was writing to in the United States; she sent me pictures and a lot of postcards from Disney. She was sending me all these little stickers, and then all these cartoons like Scrooge McDuck and Pooh Bear came to Russia. I always wanted to go to Disney World; it was my dream to move here.

I love Disney World. I love everything about Mickey Mouse, wearing that shirt all the time. When I came to the Magic Kingdom, I saw Mickey Mouse, and there was a parade and all the shows and all the train rides and the roller coasters. Of course, I've never seen anything like this in Russia; they don't have anything like that there. I mean, everybody dreams of coming just to enjoy the paradise that they are giving to kids and adults there. Disney World is this great paradise. You feel like you're on a special planet every time you go there. And I think this is the whole idea of happiness, that the people, when they go there, it's just wonderful. I have so much fun every time I go.

Racing in circles

STÉPHAN GREGOIRE
Born: France
Home: Carmel, Indiana

THE REASON I came to America was because of the Indy 500; that's how I ended up in Indianapolis. The Indy 500 is one of the oldest races and everybody knows it; it's the biggest car race in the world. It's a huge privilege to be in this race. It's like being in the Olympics. And so, for me, it means a lot to have done it seven times. I came with nothing. I really made my name here. Here we race on ovals; we go around in circles. Whereas in Europe, they only have the road-course type of racing, the regular race-tracks where you turn right and left. They do not have ovals. In Europe, people don't have much discipline. People are very disciplined here. America has great racing.

The loyalty from race fans in America is amazing. I was so amazed when I came to the Indy 500; I didn't realize that everybody knew me. I was going to a grocery store and people would stop me to sign autographs. To me that was, like, unbelievable. I never had that experience before in Europe. So I think the race fans here are

much more loyal; they really get in touch with the drivers. In Europe, the race fans are more interested in the race car itself more than the driver. The race fans here in the U.S. are much more loyal to drivers. They respect the driver more because the danger is much higher here.

They call me the "French redneck"; I'm fine with that. If you're not very knowledgeable about racing, you think, "Oh, you're a racer; you're a redneck," but the IndyCar Series actually is not that way. NASCAR is so popular that when we say "racing," we think "NASCAR." IndyCar is very different from NASCAR. The IndyCar Series is definitely not what you would call the "redneck" series. I don't want to be insulting, because I have a lot of good friends who we can call "rednecks." The IndyCar Series has much more European flavor because the engineers are from England. The cars are made in Italy.

I love America. I mean, how can we not love America? I never criticize America. Like some of my friends, my French friends are critical of America. It's not perfect. Of course, you know, the whole world critiques

America. I think it's for one reason: It's because it's the best country to be in and so I think maybe they're jealous. They criticize the American system, which doesn't mean they don't like Americans, you see; you don't want to mix the two.

Big waves

BRUNO LEMOS
Born: Brazil
Home: Haleiwa, Hawaii

I AM A surfer. Hawaii is a paradise for surfers. I started surfing when I was twelve. When I was fourteen I was already into surfing bigger waves than other people. I got really into big waves, and being from Brazil, there is not big surf over there. When you are a surfer, you are always going to hear about Hawaii 'cause it's where the best waves on the planet are.

One of the things that would go through my mind, I was questioning God, "Why wasn't I born in Hawaii? Why was I born in Brazil, where there is no big surf? There are so many people born in Hawaii each day, why not me?"

When I turned twenty, I got the chance to come as a tourist; I applied for my work permit, got a green card. I ended up staying here, got married, and had a son.

I always dreamed about coming here, but I didn't dream about coming to the U.S. like other people who want to come here to work; I just wanted to come to Hawaii to surf. My dream wasn't to become an American at first; I just wanted to come to Hawaii to surf big waves. But once I was here I saw how the country is with the laws and everything else and later on I dreamed about becoming an American.

When I first got here in the U.S. I thought I would become a surfer and I ended up becoming a laborer. I had to work hard even to buy surfboards. Then I was working so hard, and one of my neighbors is one of the best cinematographers, and

I used to see him making money with a small camera, and I was like, "If he's making that much money, I can too." I ended up becoming a photographer and a videographer, specializing in surf, mainly shooting the water. It's not my full-time job right now. I have a full-time job but I do that part-time, which helps me a lot.

I love being here, 'cause I get to surf every day after work. I get to enjoy the ocean; the ocean is not polluted like where I'm from. I just love that.

Fame

VLADIMIR KOZLOV
Born: Russia
Home: Tampa, Florida

WHEN I WAS a kid, I watched *Rocky III*, and I saw this strong, big guy. It was Hulk Hogan. And I decided one day I could become like him. Strong, good-looking. When Hulk Hogan wrestled Sylvester Stallone, I said, "What kind of wrestling is that?" I found out it's WWE. So I got it in my mind: *One day, when I grow up I will become superstacked like him.* But we didn't have this type of wrestling, so I did a type of Russian mixed martial arts. When I got the opportunity to move to the United States, my dream came [true]. I became [a] WWE superstar. So now I can travel around the world. I perform; I make people happy. WWE has very good promotion around the world. Like, five hundred million people see us in different countries. I think the whole world follows wrestling right now. I'm on top of the world!

You can see my action figure and see me in video games, and WWE has cable TV; we are on Eurosport, and kids all over the world can follow our stories. People come from around the world to see me—they are coming from Asia, people coming from Africa, people coming from Europe, people coming from Mexico. Yester-

Vladimir on the WrestleMania tour.

WHAT DID YOU DISCOVER WHEN YOU CAME TO AMERICA?

day I saw a couple guys, they say, "We came from Israel." I saw a couple guys who said they come from South Africa. Who's coming to watch the Super Bowl from Africa and from Asia and from different countries? Nobody.

If you become successful in the United States, if you become a WWE superstar or successful in a different industry, you will become automatically successful around the world. You become a very famous person. We have so many fans and we have big production. We have big promotion. Everybody knows us; we have five hundred million people who are watching us on national TV, cable TV, everywhere. Everybody's coming from around the world to see WrestleMania.

I reached my dream, live in dream country, have a dream job, and became a United States citizen. Everything's possible in this life. You just have to figure out your character.

"If you become successful in the United States . . . you will become automatically successful around the world."

Freethinkers

VANDHANA AND SESHU BAIREDDY
Born: India
Home: Sioux Falls, South Dakota

AMERICA ALLOWS YOU to sense the world of education, not through memorizing, but through understanding. They allow you to explore libraries for the kind of information that you get. What do you think the right answer should be? Not what the textbook says. They allow the students to do what they want. I think my children have actually made me feel and understand education in a totally different perspective than I've ever had before.

In India, you've got pressurized textbooks. You've got lessons, you've got classes, and you've just got to know them by the end of the year. I was scared of school when I was in India, because everything about school was, you get a math book; you've got to know your problems. You got a science book; you've just got to know all your experiments. And you learn them by heart; you memorize them, whereas my children here have taught me you need to understand. You need to feel; you need to hear; you need a sense. It's like looking at a glass of water and saying, "It's half-empty or half-full." I have actually learned education through my children. My spelling has improved; the way I talk has improved.

My kids have their own lives. They're already so busy. I mean, sometimes I have to call my kids and say, "Hello, how are you? Did you have a good day?" Otherwise it's like, "I've got tae kwon do. I've got school. I've got swimming. I've got violin."

WHAT DID YOU DISCOVER WHEN YOU CAME TO AMERICA?----

Rights for (sm)all people

LAWRENCE AND RITA MILLER
Born: The Philippines
Home: Jacksonville, Florida

LAWRENCE:

We met at a bus stop. My dad and I were out jogging and he saw her standing at a bus stop, and he said, "That's somebody's little girl," and he said, "You'd better go back and check and make sure she's all right." So I ran up to the bus stop and I said, "Are you okay; does your mom know you're out here?" And needless to say Rita was upset. And she said, "No, my mom is on the other side of the world." Then I said, "Well, let's get together," and she said, "Where?" and I said, "Dairy Queen's right around the corner." We sat there at Dairy Queen for a while and then she came over to try to learn some computer. But she didn't learn computer. She started putting away my clothes and cleaning up my room. One thing led to another; then she was going to have to go back to Indonesia. She was at the point where she couldn't stay any longer and I was going to lose her. And I'd been seeing her for three or four weeks, and I said, "I don't want you to leave," and she said, "Well, I have to leave," and then at that point we decided maybe we should get married.

See how tall she is? She's short. We don't have those barriers here. People accept you for who you are. You don't have to fit in. You make your own place in America. You don't have to join the crowd. You are a crowd of one. I'm legally blind, so I can't drive. We have complementary disabilities. What she can't say and do, I can say and do. And what I can't do, she can do. Together, we can accomplish owning and running our own business. We're vendors. Rita's my driver and she also loads the snack machines for my business. We're making a profit, even in this economy.

RITA:

Here disabled people can do stuff like normal people do, like short people can drive and be independent. Here I can drive. The state of Florida has equipment for small people; they help disabled people overcome their challenges so that they can

work. They fixed the pedal for me and gave me equipment for the gas and brakes and a special seat. You can park in the disabled spot and you don't need to walk far from your car to where you go. In the Philippines, the doctors said I could not have a baby 'cause I'm too short, too small, but I have two now, a boy and a girl. I'm free to be anything I want. I don't worry about what people think about me. I like America because America takes care of disabled people.

Rights for deaf people

ANDREW AND ELENA GRINBERG
Born: Russia
Home: Brattleboro, Vermont

IN AMERICA, LIFE as a deaf person is much better than in Russia, because there's so much technology and advancement to make the world accessible here. You can have access to college and education and have more job choices than what would be available to me in Russia. Unfortunately, in my country where I was born, deaf people are very limited.

When I grew up, my family forbid us from using sign language. I had to read lips and try to learn to speak myself as best I can. I went to school and studied without access. The teachers would speak and I can't hear. I'd try to read lips and I would miss what was being said, so I would have to look over at my neighbor and see what they were writing. It was not easy.

When I came here to America, I found that the people were much more accepting of me as an individual who was human and I just happened to be deaf.

I was so excited to meet other deaf people and to be able to go out and socialize, and enjoy myself as a deaf person. The transportation that's here in America allows

us to be able to travel so much more easily than in Russia. The technology here is what is the absolute best part. Videophones, I can talk on the phone by using sign language through my television set and a videophone. And it's phenomenal. I could just call someone, anyone, a person who doesn't know sign language, like a doctor's office, or order pizza. All I have to do is turn on my videophone and make a phone call through a video relay service and an interpreter will interpret the phone call for me. I can pay my bills online or do anything else. I have complete access to the phone system like everybody else, and I get to use my own visual language. That's the best part; that new technology is phenomenal.

In America, they strive for removing barriers and discrimination to deaf individuals and give an equal opportunity and communication access. As an American deaf person, I have communication access by means of a sign language interpreter. In America, you can go to any university and have communication access via a sign language interpreter.

In Russia, it's an embarrassment. I could not show people in public that I was deaf. I had to keep it hidden. I was very shy, because I knew I couldn't show my deafness in public, because I would be criticized. People would assume that I was just deaf and "dumb." And that perception is still there. In America, I'm so proud to be deaf. I am who I am and I love it. Being deaf is great. I'm afraid of nothing.

I'm just so proud to be deaf and considered equal to everyone else. That's it. That's what freedom is to me, being deaf and being proud of the fact that I am deaf and I am equal to every other citizen.

"Without the U.S. military, I think the world would be lost in chaos."

The best military in the world

RAYMOND FAIRWEATHER
Born: Jamaica
Home: Birmingham, Alabama

AMERICA HAS THE best military in the world. Without the U.S. military, I think the world would be lost in chaos. If anything should happen to me, if they send me out to war and I have to die for this country, it would have been worth it. I think I owe this country a lot. I came here and went to college, got a degree. I got a life, got a wife, so I owe it back to the U.S.

113

The Yankee can-do attitude

WILLIAM SEABROOK
Born: United Kingdom
Home: West Chicago, Illinois

I WAS ALWAYS impressed by Americans and their Yankee "can-do" attitude: "I'm going to get it done, no matter what." This goes back to the fifties and sixties. I always admired the productivity of the people in this country. Even during World War II, when I was in the British army, and the Americans arrived, they had smart-looking uniforms; they were smart, had terrific equipment, money; the mess halls were well stocked. They had the ice cream, the steaks, and all of the stuff that we didn't have. I was amazed when I went into one of their mess halls and I saw all this ice cream, and I thought, *Oh, my Lord, where in the world can you get that from?* We had, like, two slices of bread a day, a small pat of margarine, and some SPAM; that was our ration.

They were just a nice bunch of people who wanted to get the job done. They were well dressed, very polite, always polite. They were cohesive as a group. They watched out for one another. They often talked about people back home. Whenever they were in the USOs or the places of entertainment, they would always be talking about home and their cars, their girlfriends, their wives; they just didn't quit talking about it. And people from the farms would be talking about the farms; people from Texas, they were congenial. There was some kind of national pride going on all of the time.

America was tough to beat. Its productivity, its ability at that time to gear up all of the industries, to produce weapons of war was truly out of this world. It was American equipment that really saved the day. I mean the Sherman tank, the Dodges and the jeeps, and the trucks and all of that equipment was something that we just did not have. It was American machinery, American trucks, ammunition, technology, and the people to operate it that saved the day. Without America, I don't think we could have won that war. I hate to think what the world would look like if America hadn't entered World War II. It would be vastly different. I think the world would be in shambles; it would be a mess.

I landed here on March ninth, 1958, with a hundred and forty-nine dollars in my pocket. I had a job offer of a dollar fifty an hour. I had fifteen pounds of luggage and I was thirty years old, and I thought, *There's no other way but up from here.* I got that Yankee "can-do" attitude right here. I was free to go and make contracts, free to sign anything, to take loans . . . and nobody stood in my way. I started my own business. And it was successful. I built it up to where I was employing ten

people. And it was all-consuming. It was a machine shop, in the railroad industry, rebuilding of parts for the diesel locomotives, and it was very successful. I couldn't wait to get up in the morning.

"I got that Yankee can-do attitude right here!"

What Is the BEST Thing About America?

PDA (Public Display of Affection)

When I see people holding hands and kissing in public, I don't think they appreciate the fact that they are born in a country where nobody stops them and asks questions about their personal lives. The fact that people can walk on the street and hold hands and not be afraid of police stopping them is the biggest freedom one can ever ask for. In most countries you cannot even imagine having that. I grew up in a society where, whenever I wanted to go out, even with my sister, I knew the "morality police" would have stopped me and asked me for my ID to make sure that I am related to the woman walking next to me and there is no un-Islamic extramarital relationship going on.

HOSSEIN (FROM IRAN)—HILLSDALE, NEW JERSEY

All-you-can-eat Buffets

I love the American family-style restaurants with all-you-can-eat buffets and all of the fixin's. Here I can afford to eat like a man. My favorite is the Golden Corral, 'cause they have an awesome pot roast, chicken, steak, meat loaf, mashed potatoes, the works! The first time my family went there, we had never seen so much food. We stuff ourselves on a Friday night and fill up for the whole weekend.

DEREK (FROM PORTUGAL)—TALLADEGA, ALABAMA

Twenty-four/Seven Culture

Who else would invent the twenty-four-hour lifestyle? Twenty-four-hour supermarkets, banking, fast food—you can do anything twenty-four hours a day here. This country never shuts down.

ELVIRA (FROM URUGUAY)—TOLEDO, OHIO

Too Much PDA (Public Display of Affection)

I can't stand watching people make out on the street. Especially when I am with my kids, I don't want them to see all that. We don't have cable, and we have all these parental controls on our computer to keep sex away from our kids, and then you go to the park and you see people doing it.

MALIK (FROM TURKMENISTAN)—LITTLE ROCK, ARKANSAS

Obese People

There are a lot of obese people. There's this kid on my son's football team and he's only ten years old, but he's a hundred and thirty pounds. And it's scary, that kind of health issues arise and you don't want kids to have diabetes or high blood pressure, or all those things. It's just not healthy and it's gross.

HELEN (FROM MALAYSIA)—DENVILLE, NEW JERSEY

Twenty-four/Seven Culture

You can buy anything and do anything twenty-four hours a day, but it's kinda sad, really. I mean, if you work in a retail, who wants to work seven days a week? Americans never stop working. The American dream knows no rest.

SARA (FROM GREAT BRITAIN)—OKLAHOMA CITY, OKLAHOMA

WHAT DID YOU DISCOVER WHEN YOU CAME TO AMERICA?

What Is the BEST Thing About America?

Customer Service

I like customer service in America. Anywhere you go you can get help from people just right on the spot. I've visited a lot of countries, and every country has something to learn about that. This is the greatest place for customer service.

TANYA (FROM BELARUS)—DENVER, COLORADO

Keg Parties

You can get hammered pretty cheap here and it's just a whole lot of fun. As a twenty-one-year-old college guy, kegs are pretty attractive. My first rite of passage here was when I was a freshman in college and I didn't have ID; I was sent to get the keg and sneak it into my dorm without getting caught.

RYAN (FROM IRELAND)—WORCESTER, MASSACHUSETTS

Credit

When I got to America I was a nobody, but the first time I went to the mall, they asked me to sign up for a department store credit card and I came home with all new clothes, makeup, anything my heart desired. Then I started getting letters in the mail from credit card companies, banks, all kinds of stores asking me to join—Victoria's Secret, Saks Fifth Avenue, Neiman Marcus. Suddenly I felt like a somebody.

XIU (FROM NEPAL)—PANTHERSVILLE, GEORGIA

Customers Complaining

When I see someone yell at a cashier or make a fuss in a restaurant, like sending their food back because they don't like the way it is cooked, I always feel a little ashamed of them. I would never think to do that. Americans think it is their birthright to have everything their way or they refuse to pay.

EDWARDO (FROM SPAIN)—CARSON CITY, NEVADA

Binge Drinking

In America there's this thing about going out on Friday and Saturday nights and drinking, and really drinking, and drinking. Drinking for the sake of drinking, and I've never understood drinking as such. For me, having a drink was related to having a good conversation, to having a nice dialogue with a group of people. I'd have a glass of wine, maybe, no big deal. But I don't understand "doing shots."

MAGGI (FROM KOSOVO)—SEATTLE, WASHINGTON

Credit Score

The hardest part is learning how to deal with all of those bills. The United States has a very complicated financial system. It took me years to learn what a credit score is and how to get a good credit history. No one ever told me that missing a credit card payment, or two, would make it so much harder to get a mortgage or a loan to buy a car. I wish someone had warned me that you can only get what everyone calls the American dream if you have a good credit score.

MAURIZIO (FROM ALBANIA)—OMAHA, NEBRASKA

What Is the BEST Thing About America?

Guns

In my country, I was never allowed to have a pistol, or any other kind of firearm. But when I got here I started watching all of these cable shows like Frontline challenges and I decided I had to go check out the Minute Man; that's my local gun club. After one round on the firing range, I was hooked! So I went to the Smith & Wesson outlet and got my first revolver for three hundred bucks.

OLIVER (FROM AUSTRIA)—BURLINGTON, MASSACHUSETTS

Taxes

Do you realize that Americans have the lowest income-tax rates in the world? Americans are spoiled when they complain about how high their taxes are. In Sweden, I used to pay almost double what I pay here in taxes.

MIA (FROM SWEDEN)—RED DEVIL, ALASKA

Cable TV

When I was growing up, I think we had five, maybe six channels to choose from. All people watched were bad soap operas and sports. In my house, my kids have a thousand channels to choose from—they can travel the world without leaving the couch. Here you can watch cable TV everywhere—in bars, airports, hotel lobbies, waiting rooms, inside elevators. You even have TVs in the bathroom!

GUSTOVO (FROM HONDURAS)—LIBERTY, MISSOURI

Gun Culture

America is gun-crazy. You constantly see local news reports about people going on a shooting spree in a high school or in their workplace after they lose their job. I never saw a gun in my life before I came to this country—I associated guns with the military or criminals. Here my neighbors just carry their guns around all the time, and places like bars and family restaurants have signs on the door telling people not to bring their guns inside.

IBRAHIM (FROM TURKEY)—SURPRISE, ARIZONA

Paying Taxes for the Rest of Your Life

Once you become a U.S. citizen, you have to pay taxes to the U.S. for the rest of your life, whether you live in the U.S. or you live abroad. The United States is the only country in the world that makes their citizens pay taxes regardless of where they actually live. As a Belgian citizen, you pay your taxes if you live in Belgium, but if you live in America you don't pay your taxes to Belgium anymore.

OLIVIER (FROM BELGIUM)—GREAT FALLS, VIRGINIA

Cable News Blowhards

The first time I saw cable news I was exhausted after just one newscast. The anchormen have this nasty tone that makes it sound like the world is coming to an end. They are all so dishonest. They never give you any actual information; they just give you their opinions and they call it "news." It's not news; they are just trying to freak you out and scare you so much that you have to keep watching.

RITA (FROM LATVIA)—BALTIMORE, MARYLAND

121

What Is the BEST Thing About America?

Education

In American schools, the approach is to teach kids how to teach themselves. In American culture it is like, "You want to see how things float and how they sink? Okay, you take these different objects, put them into water, and you come home and you try that out yourself." Whereas in India, you read the book: "This item sinks; this ball floats." That's it. Somebody says something and you are supposed to believe that, just blind. You have to push it into their minds. When you keep thrusting it into them, people don't think.

MEENAL (FROM INDIA)—SPRINGBORO, OHIO

Bribing Kids to Learn

They have funny ways of getting the kids to learn here. I was really shocked the first time I arrived at my kid's school to see that they say, "If you learn to read, you will get a pizza from Pizza Hut." We don't have that in Europe. You don't learn just for a reward.

IOURI (FROM RUSSIA)--SEATTLE, WASHINGTON

what has america given you?

CHAPTER FOUR

Oprah Winfrey

I record *Oprah* every day and I watch her when I am eating dinner. She is an inspiration to me. The greatest day in my life was when I got tickets to sit in the studio audience at *The Oprah Winfrey Show*. In my country it is unthinkable that the richest person in the country is that accessible.

MERCEDES (FROM BOLIVIA)—PERU, ILLINOIS

God

I'm from China, and where I'm from I didn't know anything about God. Through these years in the United States, I was just amazed that every corner of the streets, you'll find a church. And you can get Bibles everywhere and people talk about God like a daily subject. And then I learned so much about God and how to love people. They do have God in China, but it's just not a topic that comes up in your daily topics. And in my mother's language, we don't even understand what "God" really is and what a Bible is. It takes a lot of energy to explain it to my mother. In America, people dedicate their lives to God.

XIYUE (FROM CHINA)—PHOENIX, ARIZONA

Black People

When we arrived at the base in Fort Dix, I got to hang out with military personnel and I made friends with the first black person I'd ever seen.

MAGGI (FROM KOSOVO)—SEATTLE, WASHINGTON

White People

White people are very nice because you guys treat us the same. I never feel funny being around white people here. I like to have friends or neighbors who are white people, because they're all nice and friendly, unlike other nationalities. In Iowa, they never make me feel funny because I am not white.

IMEE (FROM THE PHILIPPINES)—DES MOINES, IOWA

Wildlife

I like America because they protect the animals; they take care of the wildlife and the trees and the rivers and the mountains. They have a lot of protection for the land. In Mexico, it's not like that. There are not a lot of animals; you don't see much green.

JOSE (FROM MEXICO)—RAWLINS, WYOMING

A Tool Belt

People fix their own houses; you've got all these "do-it-yourselfers" here, people who just get up and get it done. That's America. And, by golly, I mean it's that kind of attitude that is sadly lacking in other parts of the world, but it's still alive here. In America every man is a handyman with his own tool belt.

WILLIAM (FROM GREAT BRITAIN)—CHICAGO, ILLINOIS

Tailgate Parties

Here in Alabama, we are known for our barbecue. We smoke it, bake it, grill it, braise it. Our barbecue is pulled, shredded, chopped, or sliced pork. On game day we fire up the grill and throw the whole hog on there at nine a.m. It's BYOB.

DON (FROM GREECE)—TUSKEGEE, ALABAMA

Cheerleaders

It was one thing to go from my *fútbol* to your football, but the whole cheerleader thing blew my mind. I had never seen girls in tight hot pants kicking their legs in the air before. At first, I was ashamed to even look; I thought it was not polite, but then they were on the Jumbotron and everyone was cheering and my brothers told me that it is [not] polite *not to look*; they are dancing for us!

AHMED (FROM KAZAKHSTAN)—MOSS BLUFF, LOUISIANA

The C-section

My first son was born in my bedroom. It took twenty-four hours. That's how we do it in Europe—the bed gets propped up on beer crates and we just wait till the baby comes out. When my second child was born, I walked into the children's hospital in Atlanta and an hour later I had a baby in my arms.

MARGOT (FROM FRANCE)—SMYRNA, GEORGIA

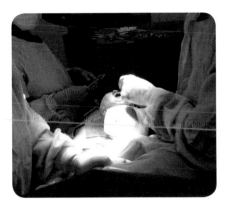

Baby Showers

Some habits that we don't have maybe that people have here, like a baby shower. I never heard of any such thing before. But we learn. We see how the people do things here and try to behave within the normal behavior acceptable in this community. So if a friend of ours is supposed to get a baby shower, we'll throw one, even if we didn't do such a thing back home. Plus, a lot of these things are becoming global anyway. A lot of these habits are being exported into other countries; Hollywood sends this information to the rest of the world and people will emulate.

SEMIR (FROM BOSNIA)—NEW YORK, NEW YORK

A warm welcome

BINH LE
Born: Vietnam
Home: San Francisco, California

THE PART OF America I really like is that they open their door for the unfortunate people like us. Not every country is doing that. If a household has it better than the other household, and they open the door so the poorer people can get in, they have something special there. And I'm very proud that I'm part of America.

When we had the war with America, our government at that time always told us, "The American people didn't decide the war. The American government decided the war." The war started when I was six and ended when I was about sixteen, and at school they always taught us humans everywhere are the same; the war is ugly itself. Doesn't matter which side you are on. So we understand that very well. The human suffering is the same everywhere. So during the war and even after the war, I don't believe any of us ever had any hatred toward the American people; we never create any hatred toward America; we don't hold the grudge. That is as they teach us. Wars are a decision of the government. And the ugly part of the war is, we both suffer. We see the American people as the same as the Vietnamese people. We both suffer too.

I feel the pain of the people in Iraq now that every day it's unsafe. But I also feel the pain of the mother of the American troops too. I see both sides and we always feel that war is ugly everywhere. That is a government decision. It's not the American people that invade or destroy Iraq. I'm looking at the perspective like a human here. I'm proud to be American.

Co-existence

CHRISTOPHER LOMATAYO
Born: Sudan
Home: Sioux Falls, South Dakota

WHAT I LIKE most about America is the way people coexist together. The fact that you get Asians, African-Americans, Caucasians, Christians, and Muslims coexisting together, that is something that I've never experienced. I'm not saying that there are no differences between people. The liberty that we have here, and the values, and the system of government that you have here that was laid down by the founding fathers allows us all to coexist peacefully.

I adopted America and America adopted me. It goes both ways. I have to learn certain things, the way people do things, and stuff like that. I have to make sure that I try my best to fit into the system, to understand the culture, to understand how things go, but still be who I am.

"What I like most about America is the way people coexist together."

Rebirth

HAZEM TAEE
Born: Iraq
Home: Phoenix, Arizona

I JUST LOVE to think that I started my life and was born the day I arrived to the United States. When we reached the Chicago airport, they wanted us to rush to the next flight and I was dying to see if we were actually in the United States. I went to the window just to find the flag and I found the American flag and it was like a dream coming true! Waking up from a nightmare. When I went to fill out the paperwork, the immigration person at the airport asked me about my date of birth, and I said, "Today! I am born today." And he didn't understand me. I said "today" because now I am alive again. This is the date of birth that I will keep in my mind as the day I was newly born.

The United States is the country for anyone whose life was threatened—we were given a second chance in life here in the United States. There are forty million refugees—50 percent of them will be resettled in the United States. So if the United States closes the door, there will be more and more people who will probably lose their lives. So it's a signature for the society of how kind they are here in the United States.

I really didn't choose where to go. I just applied for the United Nations to become a refugee. And they told me that I was going to America. I didn't know anything about America at that time. It was only what I saw from a few movies that we were allowed to see in Iraq—not a lot of American movies were shown there during Saddam's regime. But when they told me that I'm going to America I started watching a few TV shows and movies, and they showed a documentary about the Arizona desert. And they were talking about rattlesnakes and scorpions and how hot the desert was, and two days later in the interview, they said I was going to go to Arizona. And I was shocked and afraid. I thought, *Because I am a refugee I will be going to a refugee camp.* And I was thinking, *It's going to be in a desert.* And I thought, *How are we going to live there? Are there houses there? Is there a city? Electricity?* And they said,

"Yes, there is a city and there are houses, streets." And I said, "Running water too?" And they said, "Yes, and cars," and they said yes. Then it was a relief.

I was a part of an opposition group opposing Saddam's regime. We wanted to make Iraq like the rest of the world. We wished we could do something like that and live like human beings like any other country in the world. Unfortunately I was captured, tortured, but fortunately I was saved and I was allowed to flee Iraq.

I remember the first few days here I had a hard time sleeping at night. Those nightmares of the torture that I went through kept coming. And thank God there was a flag, an American flag, outside the apartment complex. And the light hit it all night and whenever I woke up from a nightmare, I rushed to the window to open the curtains to look at the flag and feel relaxed and safe again.

I actually have more loyalty to this country than to Iraq. And I'm not ashamed to say that, even in front of my countrymen. Because my countrymen, my own country, threatened my life. But this country saved my life. This country gave me a second chance at life. My loyalty is to this country more than to Iraq, the country that I was born in.

The very important thing that I found here is that people's lives are valued here. And I remember when I first wanted to go to a store to buy some groceries, I reached an intersection where there's a stop sign, and I wanted to cross but I saw a car coming, so I stopped. In Iraq, this is what I had in my mind: If you cross the street, people who have cars are in a higher rank than pedestrians, so you have to literally run for your life when you cross the street there. But here, the gentleman in the car stopped—and I was waiting for him to pass and we stood for a while, looking at each other. I am waiting for him to pass and he's waiting for me to pass, but I didn't know that at that time. And then he waved; he said, "Go ahead," and I said, "Really, yeah, and then you run me over." And when I crossed, I really ran. But then I understood that people really value people's lives. And not only people, but also animals.

Here, in the United States, they care about animals. I remember it was about a month and a half from my arrival and I saw a person walking his dog, and his dog had kind of socks on his feet, and I was wondering why would he have socks on a dog's feet. And I was very curious and I asked him and he said the pavement is hot. And I said, "Wow, really?" They care about animals to that degree and even their feelings? Humans are not treated like that in Iraq. I would rather be a dog in the United States than a human being in Iraq.

A dream

CHRISTINA BAHRAMI
Born: Iran
Home: River Hills, Wisconsin

SO MANY OF my dreams were killed and taken away from me just because I was a girl born in Iran after the revolution. In my dream, as a ten-year-old, I always was a congresswoman. I was attorney general. I was Speaker of the House. I was somebody important. Somebody who could change people's lives. Somebody who could touch lives, change worlds, change laws. My dream never came true because I was born in Iran and I could not bow to do the wishes that those mullahs had. And they wanted me to always confirm what they already had in mind, and because there is just one party there, my dreams, they did not come true. I am so happy that there is a place on the face of this world where there is such a freedom. I did enjoy it and I was so blessed to be here, so honored and I enjoy every day being here and watching the news. People debate; people express their true feeling with no consequences. That's the real beauty of the America I love. Like, we see the Tea Party movement. They are allowed to express their opinion without any fear. This is the biggest thing I admire about America. So many people with so many backgrounds. Different opinions. They live freely; they express their opinion. Sometimes people abuse their rights, but they probably don't know how valuable those rights are, because they never lived anywhere where they have no rights.

By the time I was seven years old and I entered first grade, I had to wear the scarf. You could not have nail polish, even as an eight-year-old. You had to follow all of the rules that did not make any sense. You could not really be a teenager. You could not follow any trend or fashion or go to the concert and have any kind of fun that young girls can have here. What I missed the most was, I was not allowed to read any book I wanted. Censorship is very big in movies, in media, in books; you cannot get to read anything you like. Even if you don't believe in it, nobody can say, "I don't believe in God." That has capital punishment. You cannot protest; you cannot express your true feeling, your opinion against any movement. All of us saw what happened after the election in 2009: Many innocent people, they just lost their lives because they said, "We don't believe in this election," and they wanted a real election.

If I said these things in Iran, I would be thrown into a jail and probably nobody would see me again. So many of my classmates in law school, they vanished when we were in law school and we have never seen them ever again.

I was so determined to study law in Iran, because I could find an answer to so many questions that I had in mind since I was a little girl. Growing up under dictatorship made me aware of women's demolished rights. I entered the law school of the University of Tehran, and then finished law school with so many unanswered questions about the regulations that seem unreasonable. I worked two years as a legal counselor; however, my work was not fulfilling, because I could not challenge the laws, nor express my opinion. I could easily be the enemy of God and be thrown into a jail.

The laws in Iran take away the basic human rights for women. For example, it's in the constitution, if you are a woman in Iran you cannot run for president. The fact that I could not be a judge, a president, despite studying law, always makes me question my identity and my human rights. And I want the girls born in the U.S. to be aware of that. They don't realize how lucky they are. American girls, they have to value their freedom, take advantage of their opportunities. Nobody predetermines anything for them, their career, their religion, their lives—they can choose it. And I want to ask them this question: How would you feel if you had been told you cannot be a singer, a dancer, a Supreme Court justice, or a president, no matter how hard you try? Think about it.

My advice for young girls in America is, Take advantage of your opportunity. Read all the books

you can read. You are surrounded with the books, media, and access to the finest Internet. You can pursue your dream, and you can be whomever you want. You are surrounded with all the good opportunities and media, freedom of the speech, pursuit of happiness and liberty. You can go to any school. You can exercise your rights. And take advantage of this opportunity, and you are very lucky. You can be whomever you want to.

I'm glad my son has the opportunity to live in this country and feel and sense real democracy. And I'm happy for him. I'm glad that I didn't have a daughter in Iran; that's why it makes me happy when I think about it, because if she was like me, she would suffer a lot.

Life

SEMIR TANOVIC
Born: Bosnia-Herzegovina
Home: New York, New York

AMERICA ADOPTED US and saved our lives. This country extended a sincere and warm welcome to me and literally saved my family from extinction. My whole family would have been eradicated if we weren't given sanctuary here. We became refugees overnight. We left our city for one day, and couldn't return because the city fell to Croatian troops. So at that point, we had to go to any country that would accept us like this, just taking our word that we are the refugees we claim we are. And America did exactly that.

Nothing could make us happy in those days, of course. But we found solace, knowing that we were going to a country that's immediately going to accept us and treat us equally like anyone else. Some countries just keep refugees in some old garrisons and feed you, and as long as you don't work, don't come into mainstream society, don't bother anyone, everything is fine. America is not like this. In fact, the whole refugee resettlement process in the United States is based on integration—finding work quickly, getting your children into school, becoming part of American society. When we got here, we were able to work as soon as we landed. When you are given refugee status, you have the right to work the moment you get off the plane. That was very important for us because we were able-bodied people, so why wouldn't we work? We didn't want handouts. Why should we be fed like at some zoo, like pets? It's not right.

From the way refugees are treated here, you can see that America is a very inclusive country. One who comes here doesn't have to give up anything in order to become American. You can keep whatever cultural heritage you have and still be American. This is a very open society. I believe it doesn't get more inclusive than this. You can adopt this country but you don't have to erase everything from your past.

But I'm not blind. I think that Americans should be better informed on what's going on outside of America. I think that's one thing that's lacking here. And unfortunately, you have to make an extra effort in order to achieve this, because in regular media, there isn't enough time dedicated to world events. If you're watching news, the same amount of time is devoted to three firefighters saving five kittens as to the invasion of Grenada.

Of course there are problems in every society and one can see them. But I see them from

the eye of somebody who's been through a horrible ordeal, a really horrible war, and the things that people here consider to be a major problem, for us, it's a slight nuisance. When people say, "Crisis," my wife and I say, "You haven't seen crisis. This is nothing. This is a slightly inconvenient moment in the history of this country."

For this reason, I try to be of assistance to other refugees through my job at the International Rescue Committee, the organization that helped my family get back on our feet in America. They found our first apartment, they supported my wife with the courses she needed to qualify as an MD here, they helped us get green cards and eventually citizenship. I have never stopped working for the IRC and for refugees all over the world. I'm proud to say I work for the IRC. It's like someone else who might proudly say, "I work for Mercedes."

What Can You Do in America That You Couldn't Do in Your Home Country?

Date Night

When you have a girlfriend you can go anywhere you want; you can go to the cinema, outside, take her hand, and kiss on the street, and nobody asks you what the hell you are doing. If this happened in Afghanistan they are going to chop your hand off.

HAMID (FROM AFGHANISTAN)—QUEENS, NEW YORK

Go to the Beach Together

In my country, they have separate beaches for women and men. Women can't be with men on the beaches, because women are supposed to cover themselves, so when they wear swimsuits, they can't be with men. They cover the section for women with a wall or something so that men can't see. When you go to a beach, if you're together with your husband, your husband has to go to another side and there's always someone standing at the entrance of the women's section who tells you if you're allowed to go inside the women's section. So the good thing here is, if you want to go to the beach with your husband or your son, you can.

SHAHRZAD (FROM IRAN)—CHEYENNE, WYOMING

Get a Room!

In Morocco, no members of the opposite sex can check into the same hotel room. And I think that's true in many countries in the Middle East. So the fact that you can hold hands or you can stay on the corner of the street and kiss, and then if you want to do something, you can continue your love life somewhere else. It's just the basic human function that you have in this country and you should be grateful for it.

RASHID (FROM MOROCCO)—BALTIMORE, MARYLAND

Buy a House

Only certain people can buy a house in Kuwait. I was not allowed to buy a house. Only Arabs with special permits can buy property.

HAMAD (FROM KUWAIT)—POCAHONTAS, ARKANSAS

Buy Any Color Car

Under a communist government, you had one choice: to get a Russian-made car. You didn't even have a chance to pick the color. Say you hated a yellow car, but by the time you're supposed to pick up your car, there was only a yellow car on the lot; you had to take it; otherwise your number is thrown back for three years again. So for the rest of your life, you saved up your money for a car and even though you hated a yellow car you were going to have to drive a yellow car, because that was the only car available. Now tell that to somebody here: "Here is the yellow Yugo. That's the only car you're going to be able to drive."

LASZLONE (FROM HUNGARY)—ANCHORAGE, ALASKA

Go Bankrupt

In America you can start over more easily than in Europe. Here you are allowed to go bankrupt and then try again. If at first you don't succeed, you go bankrupt and start all over. They even give you credit for trying. It is all part of the trial and error. If you go bankrupt in Europe you are done forever.

LUDWIG (FROM GERMANY)—BUCKSPORT, MAINE

Talk About the President

When I first arrived to the United States, Bill Clinton was the president. And whenever I was around my coworkers and I heard them talking about the president, I used to excuse myself and walk away from them, 'cause I don't want to be "caught" talking about the president. I used to say, "Let them go to jail. I don't want to go to jail anymore." But then they explained to me that here it's normal and you could express your feelings, even if it was the president. And that's something we can't do in Iraq. Anything we say about our president over there, we will go to jail, if not [be] killed. But here, people even in the news, on the TV, in public, they're not afraid to speak their minds.

HAZEM (FROM IRAQ)—PHOENIX, ARIZONA

Complain

As an American citizen you can say, "Well, I want this to be fixed right away." As immigrants, we have to think first, *Do I really have the right to pursue this issue or not? Is it something that's really legally available to me, or not? Can I really make a fuss in this place and make a manager come and apologize if they made a mistake?*

SEMIR (FROM BOSNIA)—NEW YORK, NEW YORK

Save My Son

We came to America sixteen years ago for my son to be treated in St. Jude's hospital. He was three years old at the time when he underwent chemotherapy and radiation. America has the best cancer treatment facilities in the world. We're very thankful to this country for saving my son's life.

SARA (FROM BRAZIL)—MEMPHIS, TENNESSEE

Sing on the World Stage

I came to New York thirteen years ago as a tourist with one suitcase and a hundred and sixty dollars in my pocket. Performing on the stage of the Metropolitan Opera is the final realization of so many dreams for someone who came here alone without any connections. Ever since I was a little girl I loved singing. Here in this country my professional journey truly took off. Today, I call the most famous opera house in the world, the Metropolitan Opera, my home. Working at the Met is a fabulous experience! It's my ninth season and I feel like the luckiest person on earth today. Every day I have the privilege of working with the world's best opera singers and creative artists.

EDYTA (FROM POLAND)—NEW YORK, NEW YORK

what's so great about america?

CHAPTER FIVE

Charity

Americans step up to the plate when a natural disaster occurs. I saw this firsthand during Hurricane Katrina. Money came to New Orleans to help Hurricane Katrina victims and I was a recipient of some of those funds. Every time a natural disaster hits—the earthquake in Haiti, the tsunamis—it just seems like when Americans see that kind of call for help, they just find it in their will to help; it's one of those things they're just accustomed to. Americans are charity minded. They like to donate money.

AEREE (FROM KOREA)—NEW ORLEANS, LOUISIANA

Community Service

Something that I really admire about this country is the fact that you have a lot of busy businesspeople that manage to find the time to give back to the community by being part of nonprofit organizations and on boards of communities. Society needs those generous, big men and women who are willing to give back to society, doing something for the community, and I have found [it] remarkable that there are many people that are part of these nonprofit organizations. People who are presidents of a company, entrepreneurs with their own businesses, who decided to be philanthropic and give back to the community, be part of an organization that doesn't pay them, these are volunteer based, and they just want to be part of something bigger than themselves. I hope one day I'm going to be part of that too.

RAMON (FROM CHILE)—LANCASTER, PENNSYLVANIA

159

what is the hardest thing to get used to in america?

CHAPTER SIX

Politics

When election time came, I was in shock to see the difference in how people got so behind a party. I'm so confused by it, because there's no gray. It's just black and white. Back in Canada, everything always seemed gray. Here the difference in the political parties can actually affect everyone day to day. Even in the workplace you see it. Where you might have a strong-arm Democrat on the one side and a Republican on the other and it's really hard for them to just have a civil conversation about any topic. The minute politics comes up, it just kind of separates the room.

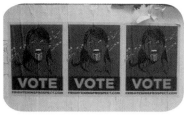

KARI (FROM CANADA)—MILWAUKEE, WISCONSIN

The Biased Media

I have a hard time with how biased the media is. You never get to hear really what the politicians have to say; you're really only hearing what the newsmen have to say about what the politicians said. It makes it hard, I think, for someone that's not used to all the media spin to understand and have a fair, unbiased opinion. I wish the newsmen would stop inserting their worldview, so I could understand what is actually going on.

JEAN-FRANÇOIS (FROM SWITZERLAND)— PROSPECT, CONNECTICUT

The Informality

It took me a long time to get used to the incredible informality in address. That an insurance company who wants my business will address me as "Dear Gerhard," I still find irritating to this day, I have to say. But informality, of course, helps in the sense that it does away with hierarchies. It shrinks distances and the like. On the other hand, distance also has one great cultural advantage: If it exists you have to overcome it. At a cocktail party in the United States you are immediately asked, "Where are you from? What do you do? Are you married? Do you have children?" There is this sociological questionnaire that everybody is being put through. That I still find, at times, just a bit overdone.

PROFESSOR GERHARD CASPAR (FROM GERMANY)— PALO ALTO, CALIFORNIA

"The Americans dress comfortably; that's what they put an emphasis on: comfort versus style."

Medical bills

KARI THOMPSON
Born: Canada
Home: Madison, Wisconsin

THE BIGGEST DIFFERENCE between America and Canada is with the health care. I know that's changing now, but when we had our son, he was born in Canada and I left the hospital without worrying about a bill of any sort. We came home without having to worry about a hefty medical bill and getting him paid off. He came home free and clear; we didn't have to pay a penny for him. And it really made it a beautiful experience. There was no stress involved after the fact.

One of our good friends that emigrated from Canada and lives in Atlanta now had a beautiful baby boy and ended up with a C-section, and when she got home she ended up with a bill of close to sixty thousand dollars for costs, and that was with insurance and everything else. But it just kind of made all of us realize that had she had the baby in Canada, there would've been no cost at all, and no bill to come later. That's definitely been a financial burden for everyone. She said maybe she'll have her son paid off by the time he's five. And that's kind of scary.

I used to just go to the doctor if I had a sore throat or wasn't feeling well. And now I wait longer, because I'm always worried about the expense that comes with it. And I do have insurance, but there's always that co-pay and the other hidden

expenses that might come up that I wasn't used to. And so that was a big difference for me. Even with our son it's the same thing. I am always hesitant to take him. And he did end up needing tubes in his ears, and the cost of that surgery was very expensive, even with insurance. Simple surgery for tubes for our son was a big expense for us. And we had to make that decision to just put it on a credit card and pay it off later. And that's a big financial burden to carry with you throughout the years. Especially when you don't know how many surgeries you might need. So I can see how that might lead to bankruptcy, and that's kind of scary.

Nanny culture

ZANETA MAHR-BATUZ
Born: Slovakia
Home: Weston, Connecticut

I CAME AS an au pair, because you don't have to know anybody to be an au pair. You sign up for an agency and they find you a family. When I went to the agency, I didn't really know anything about America besides the fact that New York was the place to be. And she asked me, "Where do you want to go?" And I said, "New York," you know, from the movies and the Empire State Building, and all this. And she opened her book and she said, "New Jersey." I lived there for a year. I was looking for affordable living and I had a friend in Stamford, Connecticut, and he let me stay with him. And I found another nanny job for two years. And then I fell in love with Connecticut. So I stayed in Connecticut.

It's hard to raise American kids because they have too many options. Like at breakfast, they have ten boxes of cereal and the parents ask them, "What kind of cereal do you want?" And you spend fifteen minutes putting the cereals together because the kids say, "I want this color, that shape," and parents will do it. In the country where I grew up, there were two kinds of breakfast, if you were lucky. Here there are too many choices. I think kids need to have rules and discipline and guidance. And I think in American families, you just give them a little bit too much freedom at an early age. But then you're eighteen, and you can't go to the bar because you cannot drink, which doesn't really make sense.

The families that I stayed with, I feel like I was part of them. I believe that they do want to take care of their children. But they have different values. The values are, "I have to provide so my kids are going to go to a good school. But that means that I have to work; I have to work hard to get there." And you get lost in the system that you work so much to get those materialistic things to provide all these things that you think that's what your children need, because that's what your parents did. The families I worked for, they had a beautiful house and a beautiful pool, but it was me who used it with their children, not them. But, for them, knowing that their children have it, I guess, was more satisfying than seeing them enjoying the pool.

You can have everything here, but you work for it and you have to lose something. And it starts with the family and it starts with the fact that somebody else has to raise your children if you want to have everything [that] America is. And the values are different. The family that hires you works harder to have you. I raised two little children and they were with me twenty-four/seven. And, in the end, when the little boy had chicken pox, it was me he was yelling for because I spent the whole year with him, not the mother, not the father. And there is a price: When the child is sick, the mother sees that her child wants to be with another woman. The mother had to work so hard and the child didn't appreciate the fact that the mother had to leave, not because she's going to play; she's going to work.

As a nanny, you have the beautiful home; you have beautiful children; and you have a beautiful Christmas card. But to get to that beautiful home and the beautiful Christmas card, you sacrifice so much. And in the end you realize: Who needs that beautiful home and beautiful Christmas card if you're missing what the Christmas card represents?

I came here because I wanted that beautiful picture, and here I learned that Americans are lost; they are lost into that, "What should I be?" "What should I have?"

You learn, in America, "Be careful what you wish for." You learn that everything costs you something; you gain, but you lose. In America you're allowed to choose. In Slovakia, I didn't have the choice to become what I wanted. I wanted to become something, but the system doesn't allow you. And you have that dream. And that's why I think a lot of people look at America. When I came here, I spoke no English. I had a very bad education from Slovakia because I was a bad teenager. But America still gave me a chance. There is something about having a chance to get where you want to when you screwed up at a young age—when you decide that, "Okay, I'm twenty years old and maybe I didn't go to the best high school, but now I'm ready to do what I'm supposed to do." In America, you have the community college, where you can get great grades and from there you can get to Columbia, Yale.

As a simple person, as somebody very simple, the steps are there. You go up the stairs and you get there. I came without English. I worked in these beautiful homes. And then I was a cleaning lady and I cleaned those homes. And then, in the end, I sold a home because I became a real estate agent and now I have a beautiful home. And that couldn't happen anywhere else, only in America.

Too many rights

NAI CHRISTOPHER LO
Born: Laos
Home: Blaine, Minnesota

WE CAME TO the United States to escape from death, but when we came here, we had to change. Here there are too many rights for children; they do not listen to the parent. In school, they teach our children to be bad. The teacher says, "You don't have to believe your parent; you have this right." But in our home we teach, "No, you cannot do all this; this is not good." Here you can disrespect your elders. When you meet them, you do not say, "Hello," or, "You're welcome."

The United States law is not the same as Hmong law. The hardest thing we had to learn is the law of the United States. We had to change our cultural practices to get along with the laws here. Like child support and child abuse. Even when a man does not abuse his child, the child can still call and say, "He abused me," and they arrest the man and take him to jail.

In the Hmong law, we do not have child support. Here the law is, they don't care what is right and wrong. They say, "If you don't want to be married to one another, you just divorce and the man pays the woman." But in the Hmong law, we have to find the cause—who caused the problem? And if you created it, you get a lecture. A fine. But, if she did it, then she has to return all the money back to the husband.

We have to adapt to American society. We have to be Westernized; otherwise we could not find a job. In Laos, we wear our traditional costume, but if I wear a costume like that to go find a job, then the company will not hire me, because they look at me as a stranger and I am not the same as they are. We are losing some of our traditions, and we have to Americanize. We don't know who we are. We have to assimilate to the American system.

We don't have a problem with the government in America, but they have a problem with us. They do not let us practice shamanism, and they try to prevent our shaman from performing his rituals. Have you heard about *Gran Torino*? That guy who did the shaman ritual in the living room? It's not supposed to be done that way. But the director does not know who we are, does not know what we perform, so he says this is what you must do? The white men have more privileges than I do, because it's their system. So they have more privilege than we do.

The biggest difference between America and the Hmong community is here, in America, I know little, but I tell people, I say I know a lot. In Laos, I know a lot, but I say I know little. If I know little, I know nothing.

Americans

SARA CUNNINGHAM
Born: United Kingdom
Home: Oklahoma City, Oklahoma

OUR KIDS ARE being raised a lot differently here than they would have been at home. I don't like the way people eat here. I'm not a fast-food eater. I think people are lazy; they don't cook like we would at home. My children, of course, love it. They find it convenient. It's a little bit too convenient here sometimes. You can go to fast-food places, and you don't have to get out of your car. Is it convenient? Yes. But I feel that there isn't as much interaction as there should be. At home I used to get out and go into the bank; I haven't been in a bank for so long.

And I don't even know who my neighbors are. It's much harder to create a social life here, because there's just too much going on around here all the time. There isn't the closeness or the familiarity that you would have in a British community. When I lived there, I knew everybody in the village, and they knew me. I do miss that about England, knowing my neighbors and going to the social clubs and the pubs. There is a lot of opportunity there to know everybody you live around. I was a big part of the social life, and it's not so easy to do that here, because there are so many people. How do you make yourself stand out as an individual, as opposed to just being part of a big mass? It's difficult to be an individual here and stand out. So there is a lack of identity here, a lack of being able to be unique. But Oklahoma City is probably not as bad as some of the bigger cities.

I worked for the state newspaper here, the *Oklahoman*. The first thing that struck me when I came here is how different they cover news. When you open the paper, it's all local. I have no idea what's going on outside Oklahoma; if they mention Texas, you're lucky. In England, you were used to getting a newspaper that was telling you what was going on in the world. You knew where the wars were. Europeans have a much broader view of the world. Here, they focus purely on their own little area and don't step outside that. They keep you protected from the rest of the world. They don't want you to know what's going on.

America is so big that it's very insulated. Americans have not been much further than outside their own state. A lot of people actually don't really know where England is. They wouldn't have a clue if you showed them a map. If I go into a store, everybody will remark on "Where are you from?" It's kind of cute; they're all fascinated, and people have asked me do I know the queen, and crazy questions like that. I think they honestly believe that if you're from England, you personally know the queen. A lot of Americans have never experienced any culture except their own. So they tend to be a lot more narrow-minded and not quite as worldly.

I think America has such an image of being the world's greatest power, of being the best at everything. I think some people are possibly disappointed when they come here. They don't get what they want. But, still, it draws people here because there's a promise, and people believe that this is the best opportunity that they're going to have worldwide to make it happen for them. The reality is that it doesn't matter where you live. Life is life; work is work. You get used to a place after a while and you become comfortable.

It's not as big and great as I thought it was. It's not what it's made out to be. I know that you can make it or break it, personally, for yourself. But it's just too fast. Everything's just so glaring and in your face and big and impersonal. It's fun to visit, but when you live here, you're doing the daily grind, and you're trying to make a living. You can buy anything and do anything twenty-four hours a day, but it's kind of sad, really, if you work in a retail; who wants to work seven days a week? And they're open twenty-four hours. There's no rest. The vacation time is nonexistent. It took me three years to get vacation here. I think I'd rather have my five weeks of vacation at home. Honestly, I understand why America's got the highest heart attack rate in the world. You work very hard here. You do get rewarded for it, but you know, money's not everything. You get older much faster here. I don't know that I will actually stay here until I die. I'll be honest. I have a daughter who's a sophomore, and when she gets out of school, I have plans on leaving Oklahoma and traveling. I've enjoyed my time here, but am I going to be an American the rest of my life; am I actually going to live in the United States? I tend to think probably not.

American misconceptions

SERGEI KHRUSHCHEV
Born: Russia
Home: Cranston, Rhode Island

I DIDN'T EMIGRATE here. I came here for some time and then I lived year after year and America adopted me. I came here with an invitation from the Thomas Watson Institute at Brown University to be a research fellow. I came here with two suitcases filled with my manuscripts. And then we stayed one year, another year. And then we found that Americans are very friendly and the neighbors friendly, the environment friendly. And it was one year, another year, and then I asked my wife, "Do you think that really we'll return to Moscow?"

I came to this country after the Cold War, when we were no longer adversaries and competitors. I don't think that my life changed when I came to America, because I am living in the same environment; it's an academic environment. Only now I am teaching international relations, and before I taught guidance systems for the cruise missiles in spacecraft.

Most of my knowledge of Americans came from Mark Twain's *Tom Sawyer* and *Huck Finn*. I lived in the Soviet society; they didn't show anything about America, and of course anything about "real" America. So we just saw some pictures and it was the propaganda magazine, *America*, that I looked at. But I didn't believe in all these shiny pictures. When you come to the United States, you look on the Americans very idealistically. It's got the most roads.

And when you come here and you see the bump on the road, you say, "Oh, they are the same as we are." America is not just the line of the skyscrapers; we have the ordinary houses, like this house where I live. And I'm not saying that it is bad, but it is something that shows difference in your expectation and what you really see there, that Americans are the same as any other people, maybe a little bit more friendly than Europeans, because Europeans think, "You're not speaking my language; you're speaking with an accent, so you are just not as good as I am."

And here, Americans want to help you, especially if you have a very strong accent. I remember the first time I went to Boston and I was looking for the post office and I asked somebody, "Where's the post office?" expecting that, like Europe, they would point over there. He grabbed my hand and he pulled me into the post office; he brought me to the window and they said, "How can I help you?" It struck me.

The biggest misconception that Americans have about Russia is that you can make democracy overnight. Democracy is the base in the changing of your mentality, and this means that you have a shift from the preference of the goodwill of your leader to the respect of the law. You have to change the law. Americans want everything to be just done very quickly. And they really believe that you can build a democracy in Russia and one day they live in democracy, in Afghanistan, in Iran, in Iraq. It is transition. Russia's now much [more] democratic than it was fifty years ago. But the real democracy will be in the next fifty years, maybe seventy years. You have to wait. And Americans don't like to wait.

My father never hated Americans. I would never become an American in the heat of the Cold War, where we were adversaries and we competed with each other. When we talk about misconceptions about my father in the United States, I will remind you it was the Cold War. You cannot portray the leader of your adversary as a good man. So you're using all these propagandist clichés: "I'll bury you"; my father never said that, "I will bury you." He once repeated an old Karl Marx communist slogan that "Capitalism would die and then we will murder it together." It was not against America. It was not threatening. My father didn't want to "bury Americans." He didn't want to fight Americans.

I'm teaching my students to think independently and make their conclusions. I am telling them they mustn't think in the way [of] good or bad, because then you will not find any answer. The Soviet Union was an evil empire for the United States. And the United States was the evil empire for the Soviet Union. You can start with this point and you will end it with this point. I was not surprised with this, because propaganda is a part of our lives, especially if we are at war. So I am saying to my students, "You have to do it a different way. Think, what is the national interest of this country? The bad politics is creating enemies. If you are creating enemies— that just means you are wrong."

Of course, I can say everything here I could not say in the Soviet Union and still cannot say in Russia. It was this old anecdote about the Soviet and the American. An American can say, "I live in a free country. I can go in the front on Pennsylvania Avenue, in the front of the White House, and say that the American president is a fool." And the Russian too, I can do the same. I can go in the front of the Kremlin in the Red Square and shout with all my voice, "The American president is a fool."

Sometimes Russians say that I betrayed Russia, but I love this country. I'm proud to be American. And I want this country to be great, and I'm upset when the leaders of this country are making mistakes and I cannot tell them it is wrong. Now I am here in America and I'm living in this country; it is my country. I like some things; I don't like some things. Now I am feeling that I am responsible.

The myth of Hollywood

LUCA PIZZARONI
Born: Italy
Home: New York, New York

IF I DIDN'T have a TV, I wouldn't know anything about the United States. I think everybody comes to the U.S. because of Hollywood. I grew up on the dream—all those soap operas I was watching with my grandmother, *Starsky and Hutch*, *Eight Is Enough*, *Mork and Mindy*, *Happy Days*. Fonzie was so cool with those jeans and that jacket, and those white T-shirts—that white T-shirt is America. Aaaaaa! And how about *CHiPs*? L.A. was beautiful on TV. Hollywood put this image of America in my head—*Midnight Cowboy*, *Saturday Night Fever*, *The Deer Hunter*. I came because of something I saw in movies. Italian people think of Americans as the people in the movies—whatever they do on HBO Sunday night is the United States.

Once I got here I realized America is not like it appears in a Hollywood movie. Hollywood doesn't work on me anymore. It worked for a little bit. If you turn off the TV, you turn off the American dream. I don't know what the American dream is anymore. I think it's just money—if you have more money than you came with, you achieved the American dream; it's just economical.

WHAT IS THE HARDEST THING TO GET USED TO IN AMERICA?----

A Dozen Myths About America . . .

1. I didn't think there would be homeless people. I didn't think there were any beggars in America 'cause I never saw them on TV. I didn't expect to see poor people here that didn't have a house; I thought everybody would be rich.

   REIA (FROM THE PHILIPPINES)—PRICE, UTAH

2. What I thought about it before I got here? Streets were paved with gold, the usual. That I'd never have to work, that everybody would look up to me. Everybody thinks they're gonna come here and automatically be turned into a millionaire because it's America. When I came here I realized you have to work hard, the streets are made out of concrete and thank God for minimum wage 'cause that's how I started.

   ROY (FROM PORTUGAL)—BOSTON, MASSACHUSETTS

3. I was raised on Hollywood movies with all those good-looking guys and beautiful people, so I was surprised when I got here and saw so many ugly people. No offense, there are a lot of really bad-looking people in America.

   JAY (FROM AUSTRALIA)—TEXARKANA, ARKANSAS

4. I thought it was going to be like the old Wild West. My father used to watch *Bonanza* every week on the Jordanian channels. I thought I would come here and everyone would be always wearing jeans and cowboy hats.

   ARIJ (FROM JORDAN)—MEMPHIS, TENNESSEE

5. America to me was big cities, electronic signs everywhere, huge roads—four-lane highways. I never thought about rural America. I never imagined I would be living in a small town, but most of Americans live in between New York and California.

   SHANNON (FROM IRELAND)—ALLIANCE, NEBRASKA

6. The first morning I woke up in America, I stepped out into the street and I looked out to the left and the right and I remember not seeing any people or cars. I saw all the haze and all the humidity in the air and I was like, "Is this a twilight zone? Where are all the people? Where are the nice cars? Where are all these big buildings?" It was unreal. I just remember looking all the way down the street and not seeing anybody, so I said, "Wow, this is much different than I saw on the TV of America."

ELVIS (FROM BOSNIA)—DES MOINES, IOWA

7. They always say that America never sleeps, but here everything closes down at eight p.m.

OLIVIER (FROM CHAD)—FORT WAYNE, INDIANA

8. Maybe I watched too much *Sex and the City,* but I really thought that people here would dress better. I thought they would wear nicer clothes. When I got off the airplane, I saw grown men with hairy legs wearing shorts with white sport socks.

ALEXIA (FROM GREENLAND)—PARADISE VALLEY, ARIZONA

9. I came here to be a journalist, because I thought America was the media capital of the world. Even though everyone thinks America has freedom of the press, all of the media is owned by a few giant corporations that control the news business, so there are a lot of things that you will never see get reported. A lot of other countries have much more freedom of the press.

VICTOR (FROM SWEDEN)—BROOKLYN, NEW YORK

10. Everyone says America is the best country on earth, but we underperform when it comes to things like reading, mathematics, science, adult literacy, and things like that; America ranks below average compared to other countries.

ANGEL (FROM URUGUAY)—LONDON, KENTUCKY

why did you swim the river?

CHAPTER SEVEN

A better life for my kids

JOSE MADRIGAL
Born: Mexico
Home: Marshalltown, Iowa

I SWAM THE river two times. I crossed the Rio Grande twice. The first time, they caught me crossing the river all naked with my clothes on top of my head. When they caught me, they sent me back. The second time I made it across and then I got all the way to Houston, Texas, under the semi bed of a truck. And then my cousin who lives here in Iowa drove all the way to San Antonio and picked me up and drove me all the way to Marshalltown. And then I started working a night shift in the meatpacking plant.

In Mexico, we had a little farm and I was milking cows by hand for twelve years. And my brother came to visit me with a brand-new car and money in his pocket and I said, "How did you do that?" And he said, "Well, I'm working really hard in the U.S.A." And I said, "Okay, I'm done." I sold my cows and my horse—actually not my horse, but all the rest of the things—and then I came to America.

I came here because Iowa is a better place to raise my kids. That's why I'm here. My kids came here illegally too. They were three, four, and six when they crossed. They crossed the border in Tijuana in somebody else's trunk. They gave them some medicine, to put them to sleep, and crossed with someone else's papers (the papers of kids who were their ages and were born here). Then my brother drove all the way from Marshalltown to Los Angeles to pick them up. My kids have a future here.

Joe Madrigal with his family.

Money

JAVIER CABRERA
Born: Mexico
Home: Houston, Texas

I SWAM ACROSS the border 'cause you gotta do what you gotta do to get over here. I was running out of money, so I figured I'd come over here and get a little money and go back home and go to school, but I never did. I was working in a restaurant, and I met my wife there and now we have all these kids. Ronald Reagan gave amnesty in 'eighty-six and everybody that was here before 'eighty-two would qualify to be a resident, so I become a resident around 'eighty-seven. We became citizens because we want to be united as a family, and also we want to serve this country. We're very thankful for the opportunities, especially to God, and then after God we're very thankful to this country for giving us the chance to have a better life. We didn't have many opportunities in our countries. First of all there's a lot of violence. And we respect the law here more and that's what we like. And we can have better opportunities. Better education for our kids.

Being in Houston is like being in Mexico. It's a big Mexican community. So you don't really miss your country. And we get the chance to speak Spanish and English if we want to. America gave us a chance, since we came here to help this country, not to become criminals. We came here to help everybody and to become good human beings. Wherever you go, you'll be accepted if you're a good human being. We don't do anything wrong; that's why we're accepted here.

"I swam across the border 'cause you gotta do what you gotta do to get here."

My mother made me do it!

DAVID DURAN
Born: Mexico
Home: Sacramento, California

David Duran with his mother.

I CAME TO America in 1979 with my mom, my dad, and my two brothers. We were one, two, and three years old. I don't remember any of it. The only thing I remember is that I got this scar on my arm. When we were at the border, I was learning how to walk and I fell on a pot of boiling water that my mom was cooking for us. That actually stalled our coming to the States. But it didn't hold us back. My mom still, with her determination, still kept on pushing to bring us here. We tried so many times. We stayed in Mexicali for six months, and just kept trying and trying until finally we made it.

My mom came here to pursue the opportunity to succeed in working here and making a better life for us. Her first job was housecleaning, helping families out by cleaning their houses and taking care of their children. Seeing my mom work really inspired me. My father, as well, he was dedicated. He would find jobs in different restaurants as a delivery driver. One thing they never failed us in was in providing us all the necessities that we needed. And that's something that really helped me out in pursuing what I want to do. Seeing both my parents do everything on their own, with a sense of self-pride, that really inspired me.

By bringing me here, my mom has given me an opportunity to pursue my career and my dreams, and that's opened the door for me to succeed. When it comes to pursuing my education and my career, I've tried to follow in her footsteps, but also in succeeding in my dreams. When we came to America, we didn't come at the top; we had to work our way up. But after a generation, you can already see how different my life is. For the second generation, we have all the opportunity in the world.

My mom is industrious. And she has instilled that in me. And I've used that quality to better my education as well as my career. And that's one thing that when it comes to this country, we want to make sure that we make this an industrious country so that we can get out of the situation that this country is in right now.

One of the biggest reasons why people should hire immigrants is because of the attitude and the qualities that they bring in. They're dedicated; they're loyal; and they are industrious. You should hire an immigrant because they work harder and they appreciate everything; they don't take anything for granted. They want to make sure that they [work hard] for a better opportunity for their kids and the generations that are to come. Immigrants actually appreciate the opportunities that are given when it comes to work. They work harder, and those are the qualities that are so important, because sometimes people here, they take it for granted. They just sit there and then they don't work as hard and they don't bring that to the labor force.

I'm very appreciative of the sacrifices my mom made. At the same time, I'm going to make sure that the sacrifices that she made do not go in vain and they are not taken for granted so that I could instill those in my nephews, in my children and the generations that are to come from us.

To help my mom and dad!

JOSE LUIS SANCHEZ
Born: Mexico
Home: Rocklin, California

Jose Luis Sanchez with his wife and Makhan Singh.

I CAME TO America like everybody else, illegally, by swimming the Rio Bravo. I was in the desert for two weeks, with no water or no food. I almost died out there because it was very cold. I was only sixteen years old when I came.

I had to cross the border because I had to help my mom and dad back in Mexico; that's actually what made me come to America, to help them change their lives back home. I came from a very poor family with no money. I was only four years old when I started working, all my life. I had to suffer. But I always felt rich myself, in my heart. I've been here all these twenty-four years and I'm still standing.

My first job was picking asparagus. I worked in the fields in Oklahoma and Texas. Of all people working in the field, I was the only sixteen-year-old out there. And that wasn't easy. In the field it was pretty much all Hispanic people. I never saw any white people. All the white people, actually, are the ranchers, the owners of the ranches; they're the ones who hired us. But only Hispanics or people from all different countries are in the fields. It's very hard work.

After all the asparagus, I went to work making structures to build up houses. And after that I started working as a janitorial person. Then I went to work for Silicon Valley; that's the main job I have worked for over eighteen years, in the Silicon Valley, as an assembler at one of the biggest international semiconductor companies. I became a "lead." And I was leader of lots of people at the plant. I worked there for almost eighteen years as a lead assembler.

I didn't plan to stay here but I found my wife in the United States in the church. I've got four kids. They're all born here. It's very important to know that immigrants are coming from different places to show respect for this country. I'm proud to be in America. I worked too long for this. It took me twenty-four years to get here today. I'm going to be forty-one tomorrow.

Twenty-four years ago, when I was camping in the middle of the desert, there's no life. The only thing you see is snakes and cactus right in the middle, where you have no place to go or ask for anyone to help. I am religious and I believed, I always thought, *Hey, I'm here. You know where my life is. If you're going to get me across the border to that country, you're going to give me the options.* And look at this: I'm still here.

The Sanchez family.

What Was Your First Job When You Came to America?

I came across on a Trade NAFTA visa for survey engineers—that job description is still on the "TN" as the list of jobs that Americans need [filled]. There's a list of occupations in America that Americans aren't graduating enough [qualified employees]. They are recruiting engineers out of Canada by the truckload. There are a lot of professional classifications of jobs that America can't fill. There is a need for certain types of immigrants in most of the high-tech industries. They always appear on the list of "needed occupations."

TOMMY (FROM CANADA)—SUGAR LAND, TEXAS

I came to provide a service for the population. I am an asset for this country. I'm a medical doctor at the Indian hospital on the reservation. There is a need for doctors in underserved areas. There is a shortage of health providers in the country who are willing to go to a place two hundred miles away from a main city; Walmart is forty-five minutes away. Not many professionals want to come there.

RAFAEL (FROM MEXICO)—FORT DEFIANCE, ARIZONA

I came to America to be a wife. That is the only job I have ever had. I found my husband through an agency; he brought me here because he needed a wife and the American women are not content to be wives and mothers; they want their own careers. I am happy to be a homemaker.

ESMERALDA (FROM EL SALVADOR)—ROME, GEORGIA

I have two jobs: I work cleaning offices downtown and I work in the Walmart distribution center. I never see my family. Even though I work eighty hours a week, I am happy because I see my children's dreams realized.

LINDA (FROM GUATEMALA)—HOUSTON, TEXAS

Working with the viral immunologists at Duke University Medical Center, I participated in the discovery of the human antibodies that neutralize HIV.

PETER (FROM GERMANY)—DURHAM, NORTH CAROLINA

I came to direct *Robocop* with Arnold Schwarzenegger.

**PAUL (FROM THE NETHERLANDS)—
PACIFIC PALISADES, CALIFORNIA**

I was the janitor on the set of a film of one of those movies where the adults make sex. They were always pouring some goopy stuff all over each other and this made a ridiculous mess.

HASSAN (FROM EGYPT)—SUNRISE, FLORIDA

I sold my patent to Microsoft and came to develop my new technology, which I am not at liberty to discuss.

NEKO (FROM JAPAN)—SEATTLE, WASHINGTON

During Taco Bell's rollout of the Volcano Taco and the Volcano Double Beef Burrito, I was paid to stand on a street corner dressed up like a taco. Funny thing was their slogan, "Make a run for the border," 'cause all the people who did ended up working there.

HECTOR (FROM MEXICO)—PARADISE VALLEY, ARIZONA

My company brought me here legally to oversee new home construction . . . about 40 percent of the homes I manage are being built by illegal immigrants.

GREG (FROM IRELAND)—LEBANON, KENTUCKY

I stood outside of a parking garage waving a flag to try to get cars to park. They never did.

EDUARDO (FROM ARGENTINA)—ROCKY HILL, CONNECTICUT

When I came to Silicon Valley to launch my tech start-up, I never thought that within two years it would be acquired by a Fortune 500 company.

MARK (FROM GERMANY)—SAN FRANCISCO, CALIFORNIA

I called people on the phone and asked them if they wanted to subscribe to the *Wall Street Journal*. I was surprisingly good at it; I sold a lot of them, but I could never figure out why, 'cause I never knew anyone who could afford to read that paper.

ALLAN (FROM IRELAND)—PAWTUCKET, RHODE ISLAND

I worked at the Tyson's chicken plant growing the chickens—pumping them with shots to make them grow and preparing them for slaughter. After eight years, I got promoted to the throat-cutting machines. . . . No, I don't eat chicken.

FATIHA (FROM INDONESIA)—TULSA, OKLAHOMA

My first job was at the Sizzler stocking the salad bar—but it got shut down after a girl died from eating there. They said it was the tainted meat that killed her—I was lucky 'cause I got E. coli but I didn't die from it.

MAXIMA (FROM THE CZECH REPUBLIC)—MILWAUKEE, WISCONSIN

why did you choose to become an american?

CHAPTER EIGHT

"Wetback," or, "Go back," or, "You're not welcome here." And it feels bad. I know that being a citizen is not going to change that. But at least, for myself, I know deep inside me, I'm not that. I can now be one of them.

I know that when Martin Luther King was fighting for civil rights, blacks and whites were equal. Here it's almost the same thing, where we are fighting so we're not just a "plague." Mexicans are the new blacks. And Arizona is becoming like a Nazi country when all of the Jews had to wear a tattoo on their arm saying that they were able to walk down the streets or they had to carry some kind of identification at all times. And if they didn't, they would get prosecuted or taken away. And it feels the same way right now. And it's just sad.

To follow the law

NELLIE AND HER HUSBAND
Born: Mexico
Home: Buckeye, Arizona

I KNOW THAT a lot of us Hispanics will have to pick a side; even myself and even though I'm a U.S. citizen, we're going to have to pick a side. People say that it's profiling, but the question is, What does "illegal" look like? I've seen illegals that are redheads, light skin, lighter than me, and you would never guess that they're illegal. You can't base what is illegal on a color; it's actually when a person speaks that you know that he doesn't speak English. But if you're going to base it on what does an illegal look like, you would never know.

We all should stand in line, like in the grocery store. It wouldn't be fair if somebody would jump in line in front of you. Why should the illegals get the chance if everybody is trying to do it the right way? You can't have the same rights if you broke the law.

"I'm excited to have a right to voice my opinion and be a part of it. . . . In other countries, you get fined if you don't vote."

To vote

ELVIS FELIC
Born: Bosnia
Home: Des Moines, Iowa

I WAS AT the caucus two years ago and I wasn't even eligible to vote, but I was part of the excitement. I was at the East Village when President Barack Obama was doing his speech and getting to know the regular population. In Bosnia I wasn't ever close to the president; they don't come near the regular population. I was very fortunate to be part of the caucuses to see what's going on and the energy of being the first state out of all the United States to pick the president. It was pretty awesome. It was empowering to see a potential president of the United States—to see a person of that power and magnitude and being part of such a movement, to see the energy and all the people being there, coming together for one cause. I'm excited to have a right to voice my opinion and be a part of it! I'm gonna be eligible to vote and be part of the caucuses. I guess most people take it for granted. I don't know what the statistics are: 40 percent of the people didn't even vote in the last election? In Australia and other countries, you get fined if you don't vote.

Elvis and Senator Chuck Grassley.

When Was The First Time You Felt Like a Real American?

1. At the grocery store, I was so impressed; there was no line out front. Back in Russia we had very huge lines. When I got inside, I had never seen that many aisles full of unknown products. I walked around aisle after aisle with this giant cart and there was so much choice. I swear I spent an hour just standing there in the cereal aisle looking at all the different boxes. I wanted to try them all. And I did. Then I gained fifteen pounds and I really felt American.

   VERA (FROM RUSSIA)—LONE TREE, COLORADO

2. When George Bush invaded Iraq. No one had the guts to go after Saddam. There was no other country that would help get rid of that tyrant. No man on earth who would help except George Bush, who did it. I don't like wars in general. I don't like killings, and I had this mixed feelings of being sorry for many innocents, but I just did the math: If Saddam had stayed there, there would be more innocent people killed every day than the war would kill innocents.

   HAZEM (FROM IRAQ)—PHOENIX, ARIZONA

3. When I went to Chicago to march in the big antiwar rally. My husband was injured in Iraq and we went to march with the other vets. As we marched down Clark Street, I felt just as American as everyone else, if not more so.

   MYA (FROM MYANMAR)—PEORIA, ILLINOIS

4. The first time I voted on *American Idol* was the first time I voted for anything in my life; it made me feel so completely American.

   VERONICA (FROM BULGARIA)—SUNRISE, FLORIDA

5. When we took our first vacation and we were coming back and entering New York, and just across the Verrazano Bridge, at just that moment we saw the New York skyline and the kids were sleeping in the back of the car, and it was a nice and quiet moment and we felt like we were coming home.

SEMIR (FROM BOSNIA)—NEW YORK, NEW YORK

6. When Obama become a president, I said to myself, "Wow, this is it; this is the best country on earth. This is the place I always wanted to be."

TERTIUS (FROM BURKINA FASO)—BOW, NEW HAMPSHIRE

7. The minute I walked into church on Sunday and I heard the choir singing I felt at home. America does church right.

MAY (FROM CAMEROON)—LAND O' LAKES, FLORIDA

8. When I went home and it felt strange, when I felt like a stranger in my own hometown, I think that's probably when I really felt like I was a part of something else.

TOMMY (FROM CANADA)—SUGAR LAND, TEXAS

9. I was watching TV with some friends and there was this TV commercial with Michael Phelps, the Olympic champ, who says something like, "Being an American is the greatest feeling in the world." My friend said, "What does *that* mean?" But I knew exactly what it meant.

ROBERTO (FROM MOROCCO)—LEBANON, INDIANA

10. I felt entirely American the morning I woke up and realized I had dreamt in American, not in English, in American—a very clear distinction. I no longer remember the dream, but I remember that I woke up and I thought to myself, *Wow! I am a true American.*

ARIANNA HUFFINGTON (FROM GREECE)
—BRENTWOOD, CALIFORNIA

how to become an american

CHAPTER NINE

Advice from new Americans about how to fit in!

Find Your Character

Everything's possible in this life. You just have to figure out your character.

VLADIMIR (WWE SUPERSTAR FROM RUSSIA)—TAMPA, FLORIDA

Work Twice as Hard

For us immigrants, we have to work harder; working forty hours as an immigrant you are not going to make it; we have to work eighty hours a week. You have to keep working on your American dream twenty-four hours a day.

HAMID (FROM AFGHANISTAN)—QUEENS, NEW YORK

Let Go

When you are living in a different country, after years and years, it's really like you are on a trapeze, and it's hard to live fully if you don't let go of the trapeze, if you don't decide to just jump into it, to work and to let go of the past, because if you always think of the past, you really can't advance.

ANNE (FROM FRANCE)—SEATTLE, WASHINGTON

Go to a Baseball Game

Forget the World Cup; it's the World Series now. Baseball is America's national pastime.

You can go to any game, anywhere in the country, and it doesn't matter how cheap your seats are, you will feel a part of something. Everyone sings songs about America together and it's all very patriotic.

TONY (FROM LUXEMBOURG)—CHAMPAIGN, ILLINOIS

Go to Costco

Americans like to buy in bulk from warehouses. My sister-in-law took me to a Costco and showed me how to buy family sizes that could feed my family for a whole month! I got a keg of mayo that has lasted for years now.

FATIMA (FROM OMAN)—LOVELAND, OHIO

Supersize Me

Americans' smallest coffee is called a "grande"; they give all of the drinks Italian names, but they don't do Euro sizes here. I don't know how they would say "Big Gulp" in Italian.

LUCA (FROM ITALY)—PHILADELPHIA, PENNSYLVANIA

Watch Lots of TV

Growing up I learned to speak English by watching *Dynasty* and *Dallas*. When I first got here, I was watching three to four hours of TV a day, mostly *Seinfeld* and *Friends* reruns, just to learn how to interact in situations.

CALEB (FROM PAPUA NEW GUINEA)—MANHATTAN, KANSAS

Vote on *American Idol*

Everything in America happens on television. I never really understood what everyone at work was talking about before I watched *American Idol*. One day, someone at the fax machine said to me, "Who did you vote for?" I felt like a real foreigner. He told me I had to start watching *American Idol*. I watched and then I voted, and then I knew what to talk about at the fax machine.

VERONICA (FROM BULGARIA)—SUNRISE, FLORIDA

Shoot a Gun

Now that you are in America, it is your God-given right to pack some heat. If you want to be a real American, visit your local gun club.

TOM (FROM DENMARK)—SUPERIOR, COLORADO

Get a Date Online

The easiest thing to do in America is find someone to spend the night with. They have dating Web sites for any color, sex, or size you want.

My favorite is OnlineBootyCall; it's all casual; you don't have to
promise to marry a girl just to get her to spend the night with you!

DEMETRI (FROM GREECE)—LOS ANGELES, CALIFORNIA

Learn the Constitution

I appeared at the INS for the citizenship test and we got into a
conflict because the woman asked me: "Who is protected by the
equal protection clause of the Fourteenth Amendment?" and I said,
"Any person," but she firmly believed it was just citizens. Ever since, I
carry the Constitution with me, because there will always be these
occasions that somebody makes some statement about the
Constitution and it is possible to show them that they are wrong.

**PROFESSOR GERHARD CASPAR (FROM GERMANY)—
PALO ALTO, CALIFORNIA**

Go with the Flow

There's only one thing you have to do if you want to go to the United
States and fit in, and that is, "go with the flow." Don't try to be
yourself. Follow the stream. Don't resist the stream. Don't try to be
different. Don't try to make your own point; especially don't try to
make your European point. I had seen so many European directors
coming to the United States that completely failed. From the very
beginning I surrounded myself by only Americans. I don't interact
with Europeans. I don't ask advice of Europeans. I'm always looking
for American people around me that would coach me and so that I
would feel where the perimeters are.

**PAUL (FROM THE NETHERLANDS)—
PACIFIC PALISADES, CALIFORNIA**

Be a Chameleon

When I came to America, I was Chaim Witz. I noticed when people
tried to pronounce my name it sounded like a cat throwing up a
hairball. So that didn't work. But here, you can change anything,
your lip size, your schmeckle size, your race—just ask Michael
Jackson. So I realized, Why don't I create and invent Gene Simmons?
You're allowed to reinvent yourself without your mom and dad
having anything to say; without the church having to say anything
about it; without anything to say 'cause America says it's okay. Not

only that, but the more unique your invention of yourself is, the more Americans will just say, "Wow, that's the coolest thing." I'll be whatever you want me to be; just pay me.

GENE SIMMONS (FROM ISRAEL)—BEVERLY HILLS, CALIFORNIA

Mix It Up!

If you decide to become American, you must embrace this country. You must embrace the language, its stories, and its history. You must not forget where you came from, because that adds to the history. I don't forget who I am. And that is the great thing about this country; it's the mix of things. I believe in mixing. The more you mix people, the better it is. We must make sure that this country continues to mix, mix, mix!

DIANE VON FURSTENBERG (FROM BELGIUM)—NEW YORK, NEW YORK

Listen and Learn

My advice to new immigrants is to blend in and learn to live within the American society. When I came to America, America assumed that you wanted to assimilate. And, in return, you were treated as if assimilation were no problem. I lived in a refugee environment with a lot of people who, like me, had escaped from Nazi Germany. Coming to America was moving from a status of a discriminated and persecuted minority to equal citizenship, and I had nothing to adjust to other than the language, which I never quite managed. My brother speaks without an accent. He claims that it's because he's the "Kissinger who listens." It could happen only in America that somebody, a foreign-born, with a foreign accent, would emerge as secretary of state in one of the most complex and, in some ways, tragic periods of American history.

HENRY KISSINGER (FROM GERMANY)—NEW YORK, NEW YORK

Speak Up!

When I met Henry Kissinger in New York, shortly after I moved there, I thanked him for making incomprehensibility acceptable in American public life. Henry Kissinger could not have been secretary of state in England, no way. I went to Cambridge and people never got used to my accent; there was always the sense that I was an outsider, a foreigner. Here you have a secretary of state speaking with a heavy German accent and nobody thinks twice about it. And I created the Huffington Post, helping millions of people get their news, opinion, and a sense of community, twenty-four/seven online. Last month alone, we had one million, seven hundred thousand comments. That's an incredible engaged community. The sense that you can be an immigrant and have a voice in this country, be able to question, to criticize that very American spirit of dissent.

ARIANNA HUFFINGTON (FROM GREECE)—BRENTWOOD, CALIFORNIA

Don't Take Democracy for Granted

You can't take democracy for granted. Often Americans just kind of think, "Well, this is the way it is, and if we don't elect the right person, we can elect somebody else the next time, or if something doesn't work out." And my father always taught me about the fragility of democracy. And you see it in other countries. Americans, gratefully actually, don't know how fragile it is.

MADELEINE ALBRIGHT (FROM CZECHOSLOVAKIA)—WASHINGTON, D.C.

Play By the Rules

One thing I learned about America is that if you work hard and if you play by the rules, this country is truly open to you. You can achieve anything. Everything I have—my career, my success, my family—I owe to America.

ARNOLD SCHWARZNEGGER (FROM AUSTRIA)— BRENTWOOD, CALIFORNIA

"One thing I learned about America is that if you work hard and if you play by the rules, this country is truly open to you. You can achieve anything. Everything I have— my career, my success, my family—I owe to America."

—Arnold Schwarzenegger

Naturalization Recipients Form Line Here

←

Why Did You Move to (insert name of your state)?

There are over ten thousand Bosnian people here in Des Moines. The way the families are set up, it's pretty much like Bosnia.

ELVIS FELIC—DES MOINES, IOWA

Omaha has the largest population of Sudanese refugees in the U.S.

JON CLOVE—OMAHA, NEBRASKA

There are about seven thousand Sudanese here. About forty-four thousand Hmong live in St. Paul, so I feel at home here.

NAI CHRISTOPHER LO—BLAINE, MINNESOTA

A lot of people come to Utah to ski and then they stay. So that's why you can find people from different countries here.

CEDRIC MAGNAN—AMERICAN FORK, UTAH

Houston has more Nigerians than anywhere else in the world (outside of Nigeria).

AUSTIN NWOKO—HOUSTON, TEXAS

When my mother and father retired they came to Hot Springs, Arkansas, because this place is famous for the hot baths; it helps rheumatism. Mom had rheumatism, and when she took these hot baths in Hot Springs, it cured her. Those hot baths did her a lot of good. Sure, they have hot springs all over, but ours is so famous that the feds put it on the back of a quarter.

JAMES PATRICK O'DONNELL—BEEBE, ARKANSAS

There is a vibrant Indian community here, and it's growing as we speak. There are ten grocery stores and about twenty different Indian restaurants. There's an impression that the immigrants are only in the big states, but they are everywhere. People will go where there are opportunities. Wherever there are businesses, there are people who are going to be there, and they're going to be immigrants from all over the world.

SANJEEV MALLICK—SALT LAKE CITY, UTAH

Officially I live in the U.S., but everyone in my town was born in Cuba. It is just like living in Havana; we have all the Cuban food, cigars, coffee, culture. It's Cuba, without Fidel.

ALEXIS REY—LITTLE HAVANA, FLORIDA

Ole Miss was what brought us here. My husband said "Oxford" and I thought he was talking about Oxford, England, so I got excited. And he said, "No, not Oxford, England; Oxford, Mississippi." And I was like, "Let's pull up a map," because I didn't know where it was. And we ended up in Tupelo, which is the birthplace of Elvis, of course.

NILDA GUERRA—TUPELO, MISSISSIPPI

We love living here in the Bible Belt. People are finding that immigrants are not necessarily running to the big cities. Immigrants are coming and they're willing to live in different places where they don't necessarily have a community built in waiting for them. They're coming and they're building their communities and growing from that. I see it happening here, where the community just grows and starts becoming a melting pot. They have settled here. We've chosen to live here and start our own communities, little by little, family by family.

ARIJ HAMAD—MEMPHIS, TENNESSEE

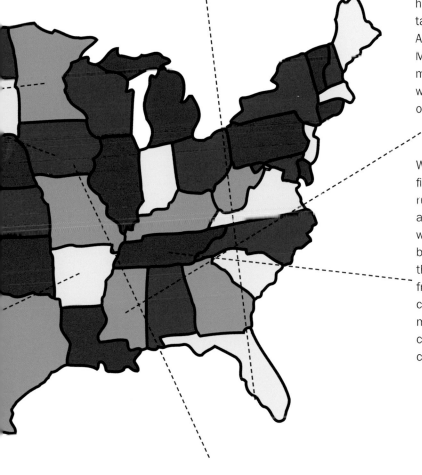

I didn't even know where Iowa was on a map. When we flew over Iowa, we looked down and we saw corn and we saw fields and it was square; everything was square. And we were just very excited. Des Moines is just like Banja Luka, where I came from in Bosnia. It feels like our home. It's good to raise kids here. There are no criminals and that's very good. I like a peaceful state with corn and with fields. If I stayed in Bosnia, I would've probably gotten married to a Bosnian guy and had a traditional life. I would've stayed in the traditional ways, because Bosnian people marry Bosnian people. I would've had a few options that I could've picked from. Here, in the United States, you can choose. I married an American. And here it's different. You can marry whomever you want to.

ELVIRA CAJIC—DES MOINES, IOWA

You Want to Become an American?

Here is how!

(Source: The Department of Homeland Security)

STEPS:

1. You MUST have been a permanent resident for five years or more (three years if married to an American).

2. You MUST be able to read, write, and speak basic English.

3. You MUST be a person of good moral character.

4. You MUST be able to pass a civics test.

5. You MUST be willing to take this oath of allegiance to the United States:

I hereby declare, on oath, that I absolutely and entirely renounce and abjure all allegiance and fidelity to any foreign prince, potentate, state, or sovereignty of whom or which I have heretofore been a subject or citizen; that I will support and defend the Constitution and laws of the United States of America against all enemies, foreign and domestic; that I will bear true faith and allegiance to the same; that I will bear arms on behalf of the United States when required by the law; that I will perform noncombatant service in the armed forces of the United States when required by the law; that I will perform work of national importance under civilian direction when required by the law; and that I take this obligation freely without any mental reservation or purpose of evasion; so help me God.

The Interview

TO BECOME AN American you must prove that you can speak English. At the United States Citizenship and Immigration Services (USCIS) testing facility, the interviewer will begin with some general information or "small talk" to see how good your English is.

Q: How are you?
A: I am fine/good/great (pick one).

Q: How is the weather today?
A: The weather is fine/good/cold/warm/sunny/rainy/windy (pick one).

Q: How did you get here today?
A: I came by car/bus/subway/train (pick one).

Q: Why do you want to become a U.S. citizen?
A: Because I love America.

You must be a person of good moral character: No exceptions here! You will be fingerprinted and the FBI will run a background check on you.

The USCIS has given the following examples of things that might show a lack of good moral character: illegal gambling; drug or alcohol addiction; terrorist acts; prostitution; polygamy; failing to pay child support or alimony payments; persecuting anyone because of race, religion, national origin, political opinion, or social group; failing to file a federal income tax return

WORDS YOU'LL NEED TO KNOW:
Habitual drunkard: person who drinks too much alcohol
Polygamy: having more than one husband or wife at the same time
Prostitute: one who sells one's body for money
Smuggle: illegally sneak someone into the country
Gamble: play games for money

Here are some questions you should answer no to in order to be considered a person of good moral character:

Q: Have you ever sold your body for money?
A: No, I've never taken money for sex.

Q: Have you ever used a prostitute?
A: No, I've never paid money for sex.

Q: Have you ever bought or sold marijuana or speed?
A: No, I have never purchased or sold illegal drugs.

Q: Have you ever smuggled anyone into the United States?
A: No, I have never helped anyone enter the United States illegally.

Q: Are you a king, queen, duke, earl, prince, or do you have any other title of nobility?
A: No, I don't have any special titles along with my name, and I am not a king or any other noble.

Q: Have you ever participated in the persecution of any person because of race, religion, national origin, or political opinion?
A: No, I have never persecuted anyone.

Q: Have you ever been a member of the Nazi party?
A: No, I don't like the Nazi party.

Q: Are you now or have you ever been a member of the Communist party?
A: No, I never joined that group.

Q: Have you ever advocated the overthrow of any government by force or violence?
A: No.

Q: Have you ever committed a crime or offense for which you were *not* arrested?
A: No.

Q: Have you ever been a habitual drunkard?
A: No.

Q: Have you ever been married to more than one person at the same time? Have you ever practiced polygamy?
A: No.

Civics Questions for the Naturalization Test

AN APPLICANT MUST answer six out of ten questions correctly to pass the civics portion of the naturalization test. Answers to the following questions are on page 238.

1. What is the supreme law of the land?

2. What does the Constitution do?

3. What is one right or freedom from the First Amendment?

4. What are two rights in the Declaration of Independence?

5. What is freedom of religion?

6. What is the economic system in the United States?

7. What is the "rule of law"?

8. Name one branch or part of the government.

9. What stops one branch of government from becoming too powerful?

10. Who is in charge of the executive branch?

11. Who makes federal laws?

12. What are the two parts of the U.S. Congress?

13. How many U.S. senators are there?

14. We elect a U.S. senator for how many years?

15. Who is one of your state's U.S. senators now?

16. The House of Representatives has how many voting members?

17. We elect a U.S. representative for how many years?

18. Name your U.S. representative.

19. We elect a president for how many years?

20. In what month do we vote for president?

21. What is the name of the president of the United States now?

22. If the president can no longer serve, who becomes president?

23. If both the president and the vice president can no longer serve, who becomes president?

24. What is the highest court in the United States?

25. How many justices are on the Supreme Court?

26. Under our Constitution, some powers belong to the federal government. What is one power of the federal government?

27. Under our Constitution, some powers belong to the states. What is one power of the states?

28. What is the political party of the president now?

29. There are four amendments to the Constitution about who can vote. Describe one of them.

30. What is one responsibility that is only for United States citizens?

31. Name one right only for United States citizens.

32. What are two rights of everyone living in the United States?

33. What do we show loyalty to when we say the Pledge of Allegiance?

34. What is one promise you make when you become a United States citizen?

35. How old do citizens have to be to vote for president?

36. What are two ways that Americans can participate in their democracy?

37. When is the last day you can send in federal income tax forms?

38. When must all men register for the Selective Service?

39. What is one reason colonists came to America?

40. Who lived in America before the Europeans arrived?

41. What group of people was taken to America and sold as slaves?

42. Why did the colonists fight the British?

43. Who wrote the Declaration of Independence?

44. When was the Declaration of Independence adopted?

45. There were thirteen original states. Name three.

46. What happened at the Constitutional Convention?

47. When was the Constitution written?

48. The Federalist Papers supported the passage of the U.S. Constitution. Name one of the writers.

49. What is one thing Benjamin Franklin is famous for?

50. Who is the "father of our country"?

51. Who was the first president?

52. What territory did the United States buy from France in 1803?

53. Name one war fought by the United States in the 1800s.

54. Name the U.S. war between the North and the South.

55. Name one problem that led to the Civil War.

56. What was one important thing that Abraham Lincoln did?

57. What did the Emancipation Proclamation do?

58. What did Susan B. Anthony do?

59. Name one war fought by the United States in the 1900s.

60. Who was president during World War I?

61. Who was president during the Great Depression and World War II?

62. Who did the United States fight in World War II?

63. Before he was president, Eisenhower was a general. What war was he in?

64. During the Cold War, what was the main concern of the United States?

65. What movement tried to end racial discrimination?

66. What did Martin Luther King Jr. do?

67. What major event happened on September 11, 2001, in the United States?

68. Name one American Indian tribe in the United States. [USCIS officers will be supplied with a list of federally recognized American Indian tribes.]

69. Name one of the two longest rivers in the United States.

70. What ocean is on the West Coast of the United States?

71. What ocean is on the East Coast of the United States?

72. Name one U.S. territory.

73. Name one state that borders Canada.

74. Name one state that borders Mexico.

75. What is the capital of the United States?

76. Where is the Statue of Liberty?

77. Why does the flag have thirteen stripes?

78. Why does the flag have fifty stars?

79. What is the name of the national anthem?

80. When do we celebrate Independence Day?

81. Name two national U.S. holidays.

ANSWERS TO THE CIVICS QUESTIONS FOR THE NATURALIZATION TEST

1. *the Constitution*

2. *sets up the government, defines the government, protects basic rights of Americans*

3. *speech, religion, assembly, press, or petition the government*

4. *life, liberty, or pursuit of happiness*

5. *you can practice any religion, or not practice a religion*

6. *capitalist economy, market economy*

7. *everyone must follow the law, leaders must obey the law, government must obey the law, no one is above the law*

8. *Congress, legislative, president, executive, the courts, judicial*

9. *checks and balances, separation of powers*

10. *the president*

11. *Congress, Senate and House (of Representatives), or (U.S. or national) legislature*

12. *the Senate and House (of Representatives)*

13. *one hundred (100)*

14. *six (6)*

15. *Answers will vary. [District of Columbia residents and residents of U.S. territories should answer that D.C. (or the territory where the applicant lives) has no U.S. senators.]*

16. *four hundred thirty-five (435)*

17. *two (2)*

18. *Answers will vary. [Residents of territories with nonvoting delegates or resident commissioners may provide the name of that delegate or commissioner. Also acceptable is any statement that the territory has no (voting) representatives in Congress.]*

19. *four (4)*

20. *November*

21. *Barack Obama or Obama*

22. *the vice president*

23. *the Speaker of the House*

24. *the Supreme Court*

25. *nine (9)*

26. *to print money, to declare war, to create an army, and to make treaties*

27. *provide schooling and education, provide protection (police), provide safety (fire departments), give a driver's license, and approve zoning and land use*

28. *Democratic (party)*

29. *citizens eighteen (18) and older (can vote), you don't have to pay (a poll tax) to vote, any citizen can vote (women and men can vote), and a male citizen of any race (can vote)*

30. *serve on a jury and vote in a federal election*

31. *vote in a federal election and run for federal office*

32. *freedom of expression, freedom of speech, freedom of assembly, freedom to petition the government, freedom of worship, and the right to bear arms*

33. *the United States and the flag*

34. *give up loyalty to other countries, defend the Constitution and laws of the United States, obey the laws of the United States, serve in the U.S. military (if needed), serve (do important work for) the nation (if needed), and be loyal to the United States*

35. *eighteen (18) and older*

36. *vote, join a political party, help with a campaign, join a civic group, join a community group, give an elected official your opinion on an issue, call senators and representatives, publicly support or oppose an issue or policy, run for office, and write to a newspaper*

37. *April 15*

38. *at age eighteen (18) and between eighteen (18) and twenty-six (26)*

39. *freedom, political liberty, religious freedom, economic opportunity, to practice their religion, and to escape persecution*

40. *American Indians or Native Americans*

41. *Africans or people from Africa*

42. *because of high taxes (taxation without representation), because the British army stayed in their houses (boarding, quartering), and because they didn't have self-government*

43. *(Thomas) Jefferson*

44. *July 4, 1776*

45. *New Hampshire, Massachusetts, Rhode Island, Connecticut, New York, New Jersey, Pennsylvania, Delaware, Maryland, Virginia, North Carolina, South Carolina, and Georgia*

46. *the Constitution was written or the Founding Fathers wrote the Constitution*

47. *1787*

48. *(James) Madison, (Alexander) Hamilton, (John) Jay, or Publius*

49. *U.S. diplomat, oldest member of the Constitutional Convention, first postmaster general of the United States, writer of* Poor Richard's Almanac, *and started the first free libraries*

50. *(George) Washington*

51. *(George) Washington*

52. *the Louisiana Territory or Louisiana*

53. *War of 1812, Mexican-American War, Civil War, and Spanish-American War*

54. *the Civil War or the War Between the States*

55. *slavery, economic reasons, and states' rights*

56. *freed the slaves (Emancipation Proclamation), saved (or preserved) the Union, and led the United States during the Civil War*

57. *freed the slaves, freed slaves in the Confederacy, freed slaves in the Confederate states, and freed slaves in most Southern states*

58. *fought for women's rights and fought for civil rights*

59. *World War I, World War II, Korean War, Vietnam War, and (Persian) Gulf War*

60. *(Woodrow) Wilson*

61. *(Franklin) Roosevelt*

62. *Japan, Germany, and Italy*

63. *World War II*

64. *communism*

65. *civil rights (movement)*

66. *fought for civil rights and worked for equality for all Americans*

67. *terrorists attacked the United States*

68. *Cherokee, Navajo, Sioux, Chippewa, Choctaw, Pueblo, Apache, Iroquois, Creek, Blackfeet, Seminole, Cheyenne, Arawak, Shawnee, Mohegan, Huron, Oneida, Lakota, Crow, Teton, Hopi, and Inuit*

69. *Missouri (River) and Mississippi (River)*

70. *Pacific (Ocean)*

71. *Atlantic (Ocean)*

72. *Puerto Rico, U.S. Virgin Islands, American Samoa, Northern Mariana Islands, and Guam*

73. *Maine, New Hampshire, Vermont, New York, Pennsylvania, Ohio, Michigan, Minnesota, North Dakota, Montana, Idaho, Washington, and Alaska*

74. *California, Arizona, New Mexico, and Texas*

75. *Washington, D.C.*

76. *New York (Harbor) or Liberty Island*

77. *because there were thirteen original colonies or because the stripes represent the original colonies*

78. *because there is one star for each state, because each star represents a state, because there are fifty states*

79. *"The Star-Spangled Banner"*

80. *July 4*

81. *New Year's Day, Martin Luther King Jr. Day, Presidents' Day, Memorial Day, Independence Day, Labor Day, Columbus Day, Veterans Day, Thanksgiving, and Christmas*

acknowledgments

ALL THE BEST new ideas come from immigrants. This one came from my Dutch husband. In the true American spirit, I stole it and sold it! But he is happy to see his insights being shared because he wants the voices of immigrants to be heard, not drowned out by the noise from those who have forgotten where they came from.

I am so grateful to my beloved husband for showing me my country through his eyes.

Since this book is about being reborn in the U.S.A., I would like to toast everyone in the HBO family who helped bring it to life . . .

Starting with my TV mom. Ten years ago, when I jumped out of the womb of network news and into the world of documentary films, Sheila Nevins held her arms out to catch me. Since then, she has brought my seven films and two books to life. Once an aspiring filmmaker told me, "There is life without Sheila." I pity that fool.

Sheila's vision is brought to life by Richard Plepler, the esteemed leader of our HBO clan. His heart for documentaries is what keeps all of us filmmakers alive. I am eternally grateful to Richard for his unwavering support. Speaking of those who have faith in the form, Mike Lombardo deserves equal praise for his noble commitment to documentaries.

Making books and documentaries gets easier every time thanks to Lisa Heller, who has held my hand throughout every delivery. She is more than a supervising producer—she is my soul sister.

Every baby needs a daddy, and for this book, the credit goes to HBO Vice President James Costos. And every family needs a good lawyer. And that's why at HBO we have Peter Reinecker and Stacey Abiraj.

A very special thanks goes to the best and brightest at HBO East Coast Productions—Heather Humphrey, Susan Benaroya, Barbara Caver, Charlissa Mann, and Rob Forlenza—and the talented HBO Creative Services team: Christian Martillo, Ardella Wilson, and Ana Racelis; along with the HBO worker bees: Ryan Blackwell, Alex Purcell, Atiyah Muhammed, and Chance Morrison.